100 *More* Library Lifesavers

100 *More* Library Lifesavers

A Survival Guide for
School Library Media Specialists

Pamela S. Bacon

LIBRARIES
UNLIMITED
A Member of the Greenwood Publishing Group

Westport, Connecticut • London

Library of Congress Cataloging-in-Publication Data

Bacon, Pamela S., 1964–
  100 more library lifesavers : a survival guide for school library media specialists / by
Pamela S. Bacon.
   p. cm.
  Includes bibliographical references and index.
  ISBN 1–59158–003–X
  1. School libraries—United States. 2. Instructional materials center—United States.
3. Library science—Computer network resources. I. Title: One hundred more library
lifesavers. II. Title.
Z675.S3B193 2003
027'8—dc21   2003051581

British Library Cataloguing in Publication Data is available.

Library of Congress Catalog Card Number: 2003051581
ISBN: 1–59158–003–X

First published in 2003

Libraries Unlimited, Inc., 88 Post Road West, Westport, CT 06881
A Member of the Greenwood Publishing Group, Inc.
www.lu.com

Printed in the United States of America

The paper used in this book complies with the
Permanent Paper Standard issued by the National
Information Standards Organization (Z39.48–1984).

10 9 8 7 6 5 4 3 2 1

This book is dedicated to

My twin sister, Tamora Brewer, whom I deeply r-e-s-p-e-c-t

Nancy Witty, my mentor and friend,
whose creativity never ceases to amaze me

My husband, Scott, and son, James,
for their never-ending love and support

My fact checker and mom, Sue Maddux

Mr. David Horton, the best "Follett guy" who ever lived
(may he rest in peace)

CONTENTS

Note: SS = Survival Strategy.
*May work for high school nonnative or special education students.
Unless designated otherwise, strategies are intended for use at all levels.
Otherwise, the following codes indicate groups for which a given strategy is best suited.

P = PRIMARY
I = INTERMEDIATE
H = HIGH SCHOOL

SS 7—Go Fish! Library Games for All Grade Levels

SS 8—"Sea" What Others Are Doing—Library Media Center Best Practices

SS 9—Head Swimming? Get Organized!

SS 10—Sail into Technology—Technology Tools

SS 10—Sail into Technology—Technology Tools (*Cont.*)

ACKNOWLEDGMENTS

When I wrote my first book, *100 Library Lifesavers,* I was traveling between three elementary libraries and needed survival strategies. I am no longer a traveling librarian or even in an elementary school, and work at the best high school in the world (Go Giants!), but I still need survival strategies. Speaking of Giants, two of the graphics in this book (Lifesaver Tool 82 and Lifesaver Tool 85B) are designed by Giants Jennifer Kopsas and Christopher Duncan. Thanks for helping me survive!

CONTRIBUTORS

Kaaren Baumgartner
Ben Davis High School
1200 N. Girls School Road
Indianapolis, IN 46214

Dr. Janet Boyle, Assistant Principal
Ben Davis High School
1200 N. Girls School Road
Indianapolis, IN 46214

Carol Faas
4617 NW 32nd Avenue
Gainesville, FL 32606

Heidi Graham
100 Barracuda Boulevard
New Smyrna Beach High School
New Smyrna Beach, FL 32169

Carl A. Harvey
10831 Amber Glow Lane
Indianapolis, IN 46229

Bonnie Heile
25 Fieldstone Lane
North Attleborough, MA 02760

Mary Hickey
6701 Bethel Road
Lizelle, GA 31052

Nancy Kellner
22 Colby Street
Northborough, MA 01532

Elizabeth Lawrie
6810 S. Boulder Court
Indianapolis, IN 46217

Marilyn Loop
3724 Emerald Bay Circle
Las Vegas, NV 89147

Robie Martin
26061 Meade Road
Parsons, KS 67357

Jamen McGranahan
4863 Shoshone Drive
Old Hickory, TN 37138

Diane Mentzer
10993 Country Club Road
Waynesboro, PA 12268

Peggy Milam
7215 S. Drive
Atlanta, GA 30328

Miriam Needham
1330 SE 33rd Court
Ocala, FL 34471

Pamela Nutt
286 Luella Road
Locust Grove, GA 30248

Dr. Kathleen Revelle
Buffalo Academy for Visual and
Performing Arts
333 Clinton Street
Buffalo, NY 14204

Debra L. Samples
7814 Irishmore Drive
Indianapolis, IN 46214

Linda Sears
5486 Caldwell Mill Road
Birmingham, AL 35242

Nancy Witty
Rockville Elementary School
Elm Street
Rockville, IN 47872

INTRODUCTION

100 Library Lifesavers: A Survival Guide for School Library Media Specialists was created especially for busy school librarians. The same is true for *100 More Library Lifesavers*! Like the first book, this sequel, organized into ten "Survival Strategies" (SS), includes tips (helpful suggestions) and tools (ready-to-use lifesavers). The main difference between the two books is that, in addition to tips, there are now lifesaver "trips." Lifesaver Trips are included in every lifesaver to provide an Internet link to help utilize and integrate technology. As in the previous book, the terms *librarian* and *media specialist* are used interchangeably. I still prefer the title of librarian to media specialist, but no matter which title you prefer, I hope this book helps you find more time to model your love of reading, which, I believe, binds us together under any name.

SS 1

DIVE INTO DISTANCE LEARNING

Library Lifesaver 1

WHAT IS DISTANCE LEARNING? CONNECT WITH THE BASICS!

Perhaps you inherited the distance learning title when you took the job, or perhaps you'd just like to find out more about distance learning opportunities. Either way, a media specialist should be (and stay!) familiar with distance learning technologies.

With hundreds, perhaps even thousands, of distance learning opportunities now available, which do you choose? With just a little advance preparation, the library media specialist can play an integral role in connecting students to learning in ways that, only a few years ago, didn't seem possible.

Teachers, librarians, and administrators may choose to complete graduate, degree, and certificate courses via distance learning. Staff development workshops and in-service training are other options that distance learning offers—all from the comfort of your own school buildings. There are just as many opportunities for K–12 students to learn through the big screen. High school students can complete advanced-level courses online; elementary students can "visit" with others in neighboring (or not so neighboring) communities; students at all grade levels can participate in virtual field trips.

Before diving in, it's important to know the basic terminology and procedures involved with distance learning. Once you've learned the basic procedures, such as how to schedule a distance learning event (see Lifesaver Tool 1: Distance Learning Scheduling Request Form) and jargon, you'll be ready to go the distance. The following glossary of terms will help even the most inexperienced sailor get onboard with distance learning!

Lifesaver Tips:
Distance Learning Glossary

- Distance Learning: learning from a distance, regardless of format.

- Integrated Distance Learning: the use of integrated technologies (print, voice, computer, and video) to deliver instruction or training to learners in an interactive format from a distance.

- Point to Point: People at both sites (locations) in a distance learning scenario are seen on a full video screen.

- Static Quad: Two to four sites are connected via distance learning, and they each see the other schools on the video screen.

- Dynamic Quad: Two to four sites are connected in a distance learning environment, and each site has the ability to view any other site at full screen using the VRU (voice response unit).

- VRU (voice response unit): a phone number to dial in to change viewing options on the screen.

- 5-4-1: Five distance learning sites are connected to each other at one time. This is most often used when several sites (locations) sign up for an event (zoos are an example of popular sites that uses the 5-4-1 strategy). In this distance learning situation, zoo personnel can view four schools at a time, but each school sees the zoo full screen.

- Content Provider: the company, group, or organization that is providing the program content. Any school can be a content provider if it teaches a lesson to another group via distance learning lines.

- "Hello, Next Caller": One site is seen full screen, and up to thirty other locations can interact using the VRU.

- Broadcast: when a site is not interactive and is simply viewing the program. Content providers offer this option when a program is popular and all interactive slots are taken. Educators often opt to videotape the program and view it at their convenience. *Note:* Be sure the content provider allows videotaping first!

View Only: another term for broadcast.

Lifesaver Trip 1:
Glossary of Distance Education Terminology

http://www.uidaho.edu/evo/dist13.html

Visit this site for a thorough, more technical glossary of distance learning–related terms for those of you who want to dive a little deeper!

DISTANCE LEARNING SCHEDULING REQUEST FORM

Today's Date:_____

Title of Distance Learning Event:_____

Content Provider:_____ Fee:_____

Event Date: _____Start Time:_____(AM/PM) End Time:_____(AM/PM)

Check One: ___Interactive Only ___Prefer Interactive, ___Will View Only ___View Only

Request by: _____ Phone: _____

Location:_____ Fax #: _____

Address:_____ E-mail: _____

City: _____ State: _____ Zip Code: _____

Grade Level: _____ Site to Connect With: _____

Distance Learning Room Phone Number: (   ) _____ No. of Participants: _____

Send Invoice to

Name: _____ Department/Organization: _____

Address:_____

Confirmation Received:_____ Event Cancelled: _____Hold Until: ___

Notes:

Lifesaver Tool 1. Distance Learning Scheduling Request Form

DISTANCE LEARNING DOS AND DON'TS

If you're involved with distance learning, chances are you're also involved with the training of staff members. Some school corporations have professional development staff whose job, in part, is to train faculty to use distance learning resources. If distance learning is new to your school, there may not be a procedure in place. In turn, if you're new to the school, distance learning may already be in place and you may find out that you (who thought distance learning was yelling across the hall!) are in charge of training people on the equipment. Not to worry—the following list of dos and don'ts will help. The Distance Learning Training Form (Lifesaver Tool 2) may also help you stay afloat. Even if you don't have to conduct the training, the form will help you improve communication with the professional development staff.

Lifesaver Tips:
Dos and Don'ts of Distance Learning

Do:

• Fill out all paperwork promptly when a teacher or administrator requests an event.

• Request a confirmation form.

• Keep copies of all information organized in a file folder.

• Discover if the person is trained on the distance learning equipment.

• Make arrangements for training (if needed).

• Determine who is going to pay for the event (i.e., will funds come from department money, the school budget, the media center budget, or are distance learning funds in a separate account?).

- Make sure the teacher has (or will) prepare students in advance for the distance learning event. If students attend the event without any preparation, money and valuable learning opportunities can be wasted.

- Give the requester an evaluation form to complete immediately following the distance learning session.

- Assist teachers with student preparation. This can be done by simply photocopying and distributing handouts from the content provider or you can get more involved by providing a pre-lesson before the event takes place. The main idea is that the students (and teachers) are prepared before walking into the presentation. If a program is interactive, it may be embarrassing for the school if the content provider gets no feedback.

Don't:

- Wait until the last minute to cancel an event. Most content providers request a 72-hour cancellation notice.

- Forget to enlist another class to substitute if the school will be charged for a cancelled event. Even an ill-prepared class is better than no class when the event takes place.

- Lose the paperwork.

- Misplace the confirmation forms and registration numbers. In case a technical problem occurs during the event, having the number is critical when calling the help desk.

- Sign up for an event without knowing who is paying. You can get stuck with an unwanted bill by not checking first.

- Leave the teacher stranded. If the teacher has never participated in a distance learning activity or does not feel comfortable running the equipment, make arrangements for coverage. Keep in mind that the person providing coverage does not have to be you. Even a trained student can be helpful for the teacher who is attempting to listen to the content provider and maintain discipline and order.

Lifesaver Trip 2:
The Essential Elements for Distance Learning Success

http://www.distancelearninghelp.com/elements.htm

Visit this site for an interactive, one-day workshop featuring "how-to" information for implementers and facilitators of distance learning programs.

DISTANCE LEARNING TRAINING FORM

Name: _____

Department: _____

Distance Learning Event Date: _____

Type of Training Needed (check all that apply):

_____ Basic Training (the works!)

_____ Refresher Course (has previous distance learning training)

_____ Prelesson Materials (Topic: _____)

_____ Other:_____

Lifesaver Tool 2. Distance Learning Training Form

WHY USE DISTANCE LEARNING?

In some cases, the answer to this question is easy—you have to! Perhaps the distance learning hat was thrown upon you when you took the job, or the hat landed on your head when the distance learning program was implemented in your school. Maybe you've just heard about distance learning and you want to know how it could benefit your library program. Hopefully, you'll find more pros than cons as you discover distance learning for yourself.

Lifesaver Tips:
Pros and Cons of Distance Learning

Pros:

- It helps keep professional development up to date.

- It can be a cost-effective way to train new employees.

- It offers a way for students to take advanced-level courses when enrollment is low.

- Students can use distance learning technology to interact with other students locally without leaving the building.

- Students can use distance learning technology to interact with other students throughout the country.

- Teachers can use distance learning technology to interact with other teachers locally.

- Teachers can use distance learning technology to interact with other teachers throughout the country.

- Distance learning can provide a more interactive method to teach students (compared with traditional independent-study courses).

- It allows students the feeling of "being there" in a cost-effective way.

- There are limitless opportunities for connections—anyone can be a content provider!

- Instant connections (e.g., classroom in School A connects to classroom in School B) can take place through dial-up connections—advance scheduling is not always necessary.

Cons:

- Some distance learning sessions are better than others (an evaluation form completed following the event can help content providers improve programs; see Lifesaver Tool 3: Distance Learning Content Evaluation Form).

- Technology isn't foolproof—connections can be lost during the event.

- Advance preparation is needed.

- Training is required prior to the event.

- Student preparation is critical.

Lifesaver Trip 3: Library of Congress Distance Learning Programs

http://www.cesa10.k12.wi.us/dl/trips/lc.htm

Use this site to explore the distance learning programs provided by the Library of Congress. Check out these programs for students in Grades 3 through 12: "Around the World in 80 Clicks," "Treasure Hunting: Search Strategies for the American Memory Historical Collections," "Working with Primary Sources," "Make It and Take It!" and "It's All in the Design."

DISTANCE LEARNING CONTENT EVALUATION FORM

	Disagree	Agree	Uncertain	N/A
1. Voices were clear and audible.				
2. Technology worked properly.				
3. Words and images were clear and easy to read.				
4. Course materials were available.				
5. The session was interesting.				
6. The session was interactive.				
7. The audience felt comfortable.				
8. The presenter was prepared.				
9. The presenter was relaxed.				
10. The presenter answered questions well.				
11. The equipment was handled well.				
12. The room was prepared.				
13. Students were prepared and stayed on task.				
14. I plan to use distance learning in the future.				

Lifesaver Tool 3. Distance Learning Content Evaluation Form

BEFORE THE
EVENT—A CHECKLIST

As mentioned earlier, a little planning and preparation goes a long way in the success of a distance learning event. Once you've facilitated an event or two, you'll no longer feel like you're walking the plank. The following checklist (Lifesaver Tool 4) will help you get your feet wet. Even when you no longer need the form, it will prove useful when you train student helpers to run the distance learning equipment.

Lifesaver Tips

- Keep blank copies of this checklist with your distance learning materials for handy duplicating.

- Keep a separate file drawer or basket to organize distance learning materials.

- Keep a file for each distance learning event.

- Mark the file label with the event date and event title.

- File events by date, with upcoming dates in the front. Put past event files in the back.

- Count files at the end of school year for easy tracking of distance learning usage.

- Keep a copy of completed evaluations (Lifesaver Tool 3) in the file for reference.

Lifesaver Trip 4:
Distance Learning for Librarians

http://www.libraryhq.com/distance.html

This site lists hundreds of places to find distance learning classes (or even degrees) for you!

DISTANCE LEARNING PROGRAM CHECKLIST

	Person Responsible	Completed
1. Complete Distance Learning Scheduling Request Form (Lifesaver Tool 1).		
2. Schedule or reserve distance learning room.		
3. Schedule facilitator (teacher, yourself, student, aide, etc.).		
4. Distribute content provider materials to teacher and students.		
5. Provide teacher with Distance Learning Evaluation Form (Lifesaver Tool 3).		
6. Receive confirmation of event from content provider.		
7. Arrange for room setup.		
8. Schedule training for staff member (if needed).		
9. Perform training for staff member (if needed).		
10. Conduct pre-lesson for students (optional).		

Lifesaver Tool 4. Distance Learning Program Checklist

DURING THE DISTANCE LEARNING EVENT—SURVIVAL STRATEGIES

Okay, the event has been scheduled, the training is completed, the confirmation has been received—that's all there is to it, right? Well, almost! There are a few more steps to make sure the distance-learning event is a success. Believe it or not, even what you wear can affect the success of the program. The following checklists (Lifesaver Tools 5A and 5B) will help you set sail on the sea of distance learning—and dress for success at the same time! All aboard!

Lifesaver Tips

- Avoid wearing red or other "intense" colors. Wear light colors or pastels (but no white!). Avoid "busy" clothing (no stripes or plaids!).

- Turn on the equipment 15 minutes before the program is scheduled to start.

- Call the provider's help desk if you have trouble during this "test" period.

- Make sure the mute button is not on—you also want to do a sound check now.

- If you plan to use the document camera (similar to an overhead projector that projects onto a television screen), use a 36-point font or larger.

- Keep images simple for the best readability.

- Avoid white backgrounds when possible. They can send "hot" signals, which can create complications and background noise.

- Make sure the camera presets are set for the room.

Lifesaver Trip 5:
Resources for Distance Education

http://webster.commnet.edu/HP/pages/darling/distance.htm

This site features a boatload of distance learning resources! You can even join e-mail discussion groups focusing on distance learning. It's a great way to connect with resources and people—at a distance.

DISTANCE LEARNING SURVIVAL GUIDE—BEFORE THE EVENT

	Completed
1. Turn on equipment 15 minutes early.	
2. Perform sound check.	
3. Bring distance learning folder and materials to room.	
4. Check room setup.	
5. Put welcome sign with school's name on document camera.	
6. Welcome class or group to the distance learning room. Distribute handouts.	
7. If time allows, provide a brief introduction to what participants are about to see.	
8. Post the provider's help desk number by the phone in case of technical difficulties.	
9. Give the distance learning remote to the person in charge of running equipment.	
10. Make sure an extra remote battery is charging.	

Lifesaver Tool 5A. Distance Learning Survival Guide—Before the Event

DISTANCE LEARNING SURVIVAL GUIDE—DURING THE EVENT

	Completed
1. Turn on local mute button when your site is not talking and an audible disruption occurs (e.g., bells, change of classes, etc.).	
2. Prevent or stop distracting noises (e.g., pencil tapping, a rolling chair, gum chewing, etc.) that the microphone can pick up.	
3. Pan the camera around the room—if students know they could be on screen at any moment, they are usually more attentive.	
4. Help the presenter call on students by using names to acknowledge them.	
5. Be ready with questions. Know who is asking the next question and have the camera ready.	
6. Watch the time. The equipment turns itself off when it is programmed to do so—whether you've wrapped up or not!	
7. Thank the presenter verbally at program's end.	
8. Act naturally on camera—this modeling helps student relax, too.	
9. Be ready to call the help desk if program cuts off or the sound is lost. Distance learning equipment is increasingly reliable, but it's always best to be prepared.	
10. When speaking, look at the camera, not at the television screen.	

Lifesaver Tool 5B. Distance Learning Survival Guide—During the Event

AFTER THE DISTANCE LEARNING EVENT—FOLLOW-UPS

Hopefully, the distance-learning event was a huge success. With any luck, you've witnessed firsthand the power of distance learning as an important educational tool, and you can't wait to facilitate another event. Whether or not the event was a total success, there are still some loose ends to tie up. So grab that rope, and let's dock the distance learning boat until the next adventure—Lifesaver Tool 6 will help!

Lifesaver Tips

- If the event was a success, tell people about it! If you're in charge of distance learning, you'll want to promote it. Word of mouth is the best PR you can get.

- If the event wasn't a success, talk to the teacher or person who requested the event. Determine what could have been done differently to make the program work. Was the problem with the content provider or the students?

- If a technical difficulty occurred during the program, enlist help from your technical support team to ensure the same thing doesn't happen again. In some cases, the problem can't be prevented, but in others a "tune-up" can help.

- Send or fax the evaluation form to the content provider. Be honest and candid.

- If the program was of poor quality, ask for a refund. Two or three times, a provider has cancelled an invoice for me because the presenter was ill prepared. You don't know until you try!

- Turn off all equipment.

- Close up and secure the room.

- Fully charge the remote so the battery is prepared for the next event.

- Notify your custodial staff if chairs or tables need to be resituated.

Lifesaver Trip 6:
Issues in Distance Learning

http://carbon.cudenver.edu/~lsherry/pubs/issues.html

A companion to *Needs Assessment for Distance Education* by L. Sherry (1995), this site offers an in-depth look at distance learning, including procedures, policy, and management issues.

DISTANCE LEARNING SURVIVAL GUIDE—AFTER THE EVENT	
	Completed
1. Distribute follow-up materials from the presenter, if any.	
2. Fax completed evaluation form and keep a file copy.	
3. Send a thank you note to the presenter or content provider.	
4. Follow up with the teacher about the program.	
5. Receive and distribute the invoice to the appropriate party.	

Lifesaver Tool 6. Distance Learning Survival Guide—After the Event

PAM'S PICKS: TOP TEN DISTANCE LEARNING RESOURCES

Whether you're new at distance learning or have set sail over distance learning horizons many a time, it's helpful to have quality, highly reviewed resources. The Lifesaver Tips that follow include an annotated list of ten "must haves" for your professional library shelves. The "Pam's Pick" blank form (Lifesaver Tool 7) is for you (or your colleagues) to complete when they dive into their own distance learning library. Note that all book prices do not include shipping and handling. (By the way, Barnes & Noble's Web site and Amazon.com offer free shipping if you purchase a certain number of books!)

Lifesaver Tips

- Pam's Pick #1

The McGraw-Hill Handbook of Distance Learning by Alan G. Chute et al.
Publisher: McGraw-Hill (1999)
Price: $27.97 (amazon.com)
$31.96 (barnesandnoble.com)
Covers issues of planning and implementing distance learning programs in a step-by-step how-to format.

- Pam's Pick #2

Digital Classroom: How Technology Is Changing the Way We Teach by David T. Gordon
Publisher: Harvard Education Letter (2000)
Price: $21.95 (amazon.com)
$21.95 (barnesandnoble.com)
This report focuses on the rewards and challenges involved with integrating distance learning technologies into the school's curriculum. The text covers professional development issues and includes editorials from technology experts and educators.

- Pam's Pick #3

  Distance Learning Online for Dummies by Nancy Stevenson
  Publisher: John Wiley & Sons (2000)
  Price: $13.99 (amazon.com)
        $17.99 (barnesandnoble.com)
      This book includes everything from the basics (connecting to the Internet and using personal computers) to directories of online learning programs.

- Pam's Pick #4

  Distance Learning Technologies: Issues, Trends and Opportunities by Linda K. Lau et al.
  Publisher: Idea Group Publishing (2000)
  Price: $45.47 (amazon.com)
        $41.98 (barnesandnoble.com)
      This book covers the history of distance learning programs and provides an in-depth look at the technologies involved as well as implementation suggestions.

- Pam's Pick #5

  Distance Learning by Chandra Mohan Mehrotra et al.
  Publisher: Sage Publications (2001)
  Price: $74.20 (amazon.com)
        $80.95 (barnesandnoble.com)
      Three faculty members provide tips for designing, implementing, and evaluating distance learning programs. Although research based, the book is highly readable and includes student and teacher experiences with distance learning environments. Its nonbiased approach also includes shortcomings of distance learning.

- Pam's Pick #6

  Distance Learning: The Essential Guide by Marcia L. Williams et al.
  Publisher: Sage Publications (1998)
  Price: $47.95 (amazon.com)
        $47.95 (barnesandnoble.com)
      While somewhat costly, I believe you'll find this book is true to it's name—essential. In a clear, concise style, this practical book covers all aspects of distance learning. Tear-out worksheets and checklists effectively help the reader organize and implement distance learning events.

- Pam's Pick #7

  New Virtual Field Trips by Gail Cooper and Garry Cooper
  Publisher: Libraries Unlimited (2001)
  Price: $27.50 (amazon.com)
        $27.50 (barnesandnoble.com)
      This book, a sequel to *More Virtual Field Trips*, includes 440 fully annotated Web sites of exciting, educational Internet field trips. The curricular tie-ins and standards-based approach make it a distance learning must-have (K–12).

- Pam's Pick #8

  Bears' Guide to Earning Degrees by Distance Learning by John Bear
  Publisher: Ten Speed Press (2000)
  Price: $20.97 (amazon.com)
      $23.96 (barnesandnoble.com)
  The fact that this book is in its thirteenth edition says it all. Bear is the leading expert on providing alternatives for college-bound students who have no desire to sit behind ivy-covered walls. It's an informative, highly useful guide to nontraditional degrees.

- Pam's Pick #9

  Building Learning Communities in Cyberspace by Rena M. Palloff and Keith Pratt
  Publisher: Jossey Bass (1999)
  Price: $32.00 (amazon.com)
      $32.00 (barnesandnoble.com)
  Thoroughly explains how to create a virtual classroom environment in a practical, hands-on manner.

- Pam's Pick #10

  Teaching and Learning at a Distance by Michael R. Simonson et al.
  Publisher: Prentice Hall (1999)
  Price: $44.00 (amazon.com)
      $44.00 (barnesandnoble.com)
  Designed for distance learning educators, facilitators, and administrators, this hands-on book begins with the theoretical background of distance learning and moves into applications and strategies.

Lifesaver Trip 7:
The Distance Learning "Getting Started" Booklist

http://pages.prodigy.com/PAUM88A/

At this site, you'll find a four-part series recommended for beginning distance learning users. The frequently asked questions (FAQs) format is easy to scan, so you can go as deep (or as shallow!) as you want.

PAM'S PICK BOOK FORM	
Title	
Publisher	
Copyright	
Price	
Annotation	

Lifesaver Tool 7. Pam's Pick Book Form

SURF'S UP FOR DISTANCE LEARNING LINKS

Once you've learned the ropes of distance learning and no longer feel like you're swimming in an ocean full of sharks, you'll want to locate your own distance learning programs to suit your own school's needs. If you're an experienced Internet surfer, catch a wave to the next chapter. If you're new to the Internet, hold on and get ready for an exciting ride! When you catch a wave (oops, I mean a site!), keep it handy by using Lifesaver Tool 8.

Lifesaver Tips:
The Surfer's Guide to Distance Learning Links

1. Log on to the Internet (in my case, I double-click on Internet Explorer). Go to a search engine (I prefer Google: http://www.google.com/).

2. Type in your topic (e.g., How to Use Distance Learning Equipment and Public Schools). Note the number of hits the search engine has found (I found 227,000 matches!).

3. Revise your search, if necessary (e.g., How to Manage a Distance Learning Event for an Elementary School).

4. Note the number of hits found (this search found only 14,000 matches).

5. Be as specific as possible to limit the amount of hits you receive.

6. Scan through "hit list." Click on blue links if a site appears relevant to your interests.

7. Use the back arrow (top left of screen) to navigate back to the list.

Repeat these steps until you find the information you need.

Lifesaver Trip 8:
Percent of Schools with Distance Learning Capabilities

http://www.state.nj.us/njded/techno/survey/results/

This 1999 survey from New Jersey showed that 42 percent of schools in that state had distance learning capabilities! How does your state rank? To find out, contact the Distance Learning Resource Network (http://www.dlrn.org).

INTERNET REFERENCE CARD

\# _____

SOURCE: _____

HTTP ADDRESS: _____

_____

DATE OF SOURCE:_____

DATE OF SEARCHING: _____

AUTHOR'S LAST NAME: _____

AUTHOR'S FIRST NAME: _____

SOURCE TITLE: _____

_____

VERSION/FILE NUMBER: _____

INTERNET REFERENCE CARD

\# _____

SOURCE: _____

HTTP ADDRESS: _____

_____

DATE OF SOURCE:_____

DATE OF SEARCHING: _____

AUTHOR'S LAST NAME: _____

AUTHOR'S FIRST NAME: _____

SOURCE TITLE: _____

_____

VERSION/FILE NUMBER: _____

Lifesaver Tool 8. Sample Internet Reference Cards

LEARNING FROM A DISTANCE—PROFESSIONAL DEVELOPMENT

Over the years, the number of professional development opportunities available online has grown tremendously. Don't throw your line in just anywhere—use Lifesaver Tool 9 to help you decide which professional development opportunity is—or isn't—for you.

Lifesaver Tips:
High Five—Professional Development Resources

1. *Bears' Guide to the Best Education Degrees by Distance Learning* (John Bear et al.)

    Publisher: Ten Speed Press (2001)
    Price: $10.47 (amazon.com)
           $13.45 (barnesandnoble.com)
        Whether you're getting your first teacher's license, want a master's degree, need a certificate to teach an additional subject, or imagine a doctorate in your future, this resource has all you need to complete coursework at your own time and at your own pace. Dive in!

2. TEAMS Distance Learning Site

    URL: http://teams.lacoe.edu/
        Click on the "Professional Development" link for a multitude of great resources. Other links, such as "K–12 Lessons & Web Sites" and "Standards & Assessment," are also worth going below the surface to explore.

3. Distance Learning Resource Network—How to Find Online Courses

    URL: http://www.dlrn.org/educ/how.html
        Click here for one-stop shopping for distance learning. The "For Educators" link includes a treasure chest of teacher resources, including "100 Sites for Exploring Online Professional Development."

4. Community Learning Network

   URL: http://www.cln.org/cln.html
   This site is specifically designed to help K–12 teachers integrate technology into their classroom lessons. Using this site as a starting point, you'll be able to access more than 5,800 annotated links to sites containing free resources are accessible by either theme or keyword search. Users can join the Network Nuggets listserv to find more technology resources. Links to online professional development are well worth diving into!

5. Teach-nology.com

   URL: http://www.teach-nology.com/teachers/distance_learning/
   Drowning in the sea of technology? Swim to the surface and click on the "Learn to Use Technology in the Classroom" link. From there, you can either browse through tutorials on dozens of technology-related issues (distance learning is there!) or "Ask a Technology Expert" to get personal feedback! Wow!

Lifesaver Trip 9:
Teach-Nology.com Monthly Motivator

http://www.teach-nology.com/motivator

This site features an impressive multimedia presentation to motivate you to utilize computers in the classroom. Themes change monthly; the month I viewed featured what could be done in a "one-computer classroom." Although slow to load, the motivator is worth the wait.

PROFESSIONAL DEVELOPMENT COMPARISON CHART

	Low	Medium	High
1. Program is fully accredited.			
2. Recommendations are provided.			
3. Cost is reasonable.			
4. Orientation training for learner is included.			
5. Technical support is available twenty-four hours a day, seven days a week.			
6. Adequate time line to complete course.			
7. Instructor's background is commendable.			
8. Learning goals are clearly defined.			
9. Evaluation feedback will be encouraged.			
10. A variety of media will be used in course.			

Lifesaver Tool 9. Professional Development Comparison Chart

DISTANCE LEARNING PANEL—EXPERTS SPEAK OUT!

For this last section on distance learning, I wanted to set sail and talk to an expert who has already gotten her feet wet in the sea of distance learning. You'll find out the good, the bad, and the ugly (believe it or not!) on distance learning.

Lifesaver Trip 10:
Cybersnax Professional Development Registration Form

http://www.ciesc.org/SeriesRegistration.asp

Go online to register for one of these professional development courses! Surf's Up!

LIBBY'S LIFESAVERS:
10 DISTANCE LEARNING SURVIVAL STRATEGIES

1. Identify a Topic
   - ☑ Think Globally.

2. Plan, Plan, Plan
   - ☑ Allow a minimum of 3 to 4 weeks for best results.
   - ☑ Decide on the best date and time.
   - ☑ Make sure the room is available.
   - ☑ Make special arrangements with the content provider, if needed.
   - ☑ Select students (entire class, part of a class, multiple classes—it's up to you!)

3. Compile Lesson Plans
   - ☑ Some sessions will send handouts, hands-on materials, or even complete lesson plans to you in advance.

4. Prepare Students
   - ☑ Discuss "netiquette."
   - ☑ Discuss the purpose of the program.
   - ☑ Describe the technology (yes, they really can see and hear you!).
   - ☑ Have students prepare questions in advance.

5. Test Equipment
   - ☑ Play around with the equipment before the session—you can't break it!
   - ☑ Set up an interactive test session to ensure equipment is working properly.
   - ☑ Train students to run the equipment.

6. Call for Help!
   - ☑ If you have trouble, call the help desk—that's what they're there for.
   - ☑ Call the content provider and ask questions.

7. Follow Up
   - ☑ Fill out the session evaluation.
   - ☑ Be honest—this is how content providers improve.

8. Always Have a Plan B!
   - ☑ As great as technology is, it isn't foolproof!

9. Model Active Learning
   - ☑ Use distance learning yourself for your own professional development.

10. Have fun!

Lifesaver Tool 10. Libby's Lifesavers

SS 2

ALL ABOARD!
EXCEEDING THE STANDARDS

A STANDARD ABOVE: WHAT ARE THE STANDARDS, ANYWAY?

Standards, standards, standards! Every time you turn around, someone is saying the "S" word! Simply knowing the standards is no longer enough—in today's world of high stakes testing and accountability, the media specialist is now responsible to know—and implement—the standards on a regular basis. Chances are you, like me, were already implementing standards and teaching quality lessons, but you just weren't as intentional as you could be. Lifesaver Tool 11 helps you with the first step of knowing who and what; Lifesaver Tool 12 takes care of the why.

Lifesaver Tips

- The first set of standards I'll discuss are the Information Literacy Standards.

- The Information Literacy Standards are trademarked by the American Library Association (ALA) and the Association for Educational Communications and Technology (AECT).

- The nine Information Literacy Standards are also contained in the book *Information Power: Building Partnerships for Learning* (1998).

- The nine Information Literacy Standards are broken into three categories: Information Literacy, Independent Learning, and Social Responsibility.

- The three Information Literacy standards focus on accessing, evaluating, and using information.

- The three Independent Learning standards focus on how well the student *independently* seeks, delves into, and critiques the information found.

- The Social Responsibility standards focus on the responsibility the user of information shows and models while accessing information.

Lifesaver Trip 11:
Information Literacy Standards—Online Version

http://www.ala.org/aasl/ip_nine.html

Dive into the ALA's site—it's a true lifesaver!

INFORMATION LITERACY IS A LIFESAVER!

From *Information Power*
The Nine Information Literacy Standards for Student Learning

Information Literacy

Standard 1: The student who is information literate accesses information efficiently and effectively.

Standard 2: The student who is information literate evaluates information critically and competently.

Standard 3: The student who is information literate uses information accurately and creatively.

Independent Learning

Standard 4: The student who is an independent learner is information literate and pursues information related to personal interests.

Standard 5: The student who is an independent learner is information literate and appreciates literature and other creative expressions of information.

Standard 6: The student who is an independent learner is information literate and strives for excellence in information seeking and knowledge generation.

Social Responsibility

Standard 7: The student who contributes positively to the learning community and to society is information literate and recognizes the importance of information to a democratic society.

Standard 8: The student who contributes positively to the learning community and to society is information literate and practices ethical behavior in regard to information and information technology.

Standard 9: The student who contributes positively to the learning community and to society is information literate and participates effectively in groups to pursue and generate information.

Note: Order *Information Power* by phone at 1-866 SHOP ALA (1-866-746-7252).

Lifesaver Tool 11: Information Literacy Standards

Your "Standard" Checklist

Now that you know what the standards are and who came up with them, it's time to become a little more intentional about when you use them. You're already an awesome teacher-librarian (pat, pat yourself on the back!), now just keep track of when you use each standard on the checklist (Lifesaver Tool 12A).

Lifesaver Tips

- Run off plenty of checklists at the beginning of each year (use a fun color instead of your "standard" white so that the form catches your attention!).

- Make a file and label it "Standards Checklists—Blank."

- Make another file and label it "Standards Checklists—Completed."

- When each checklist fills up, file it in the appropriate file.

- Throughout the year, whenever you have a spare moment (like there is one!), check over the checklists to see if all of the standards are being covered.

- At the end of the year, do a quick tally (Lifesaver 12B) to include in your Annual Report.

Lifesaver Trip 12:
Marco Polo Internet Home Page

http://marcopolo.worldcom.com/

The MarcoPolo program hosts free, standards-based Internet content for the K–12 teachers and classes.

INFORMATION LITERACY STANDARDS CHECKLIST

FOR THE WEEK OF _____

Lesson Title	ILS 1 Assesses	ILS 2 Evaluates	ILS 3 Uses	ILS 4 Pursues	ILS 5 Appreciates	ILS 6 Strives	ILS 7 Understands	ILS 8 Respects	ILS 9 Models

Lifesaver Tool 12A. Information Literacy Standards Checklist

INFORMATION LITERACY STANDARDS
TALLY SHEET

Information Literacy Standards	Total Times Used _____ Semester/Year
ILS 1: Assesses	
ILS 2: Evaluates	
ILS 3: Uses	
ILS 4: Pursues	
ILS 5: Appreciates	
ILS 6: Strives	
ILS 7: Understands	
ILS 8: Respects	
ILS 9: Models	

Lifesaver Tool 12B. Information Literacy Standards Tally Sheet

STRATEGY SURVIVAL GUIDE

When you start looking at the standards, it's easy to get confused! For example, you may be wondering just what the difference is among "respect," "understand," and "appreciate." After reviewing a few of the examples in Lifesaver Tool 13, I think your understanding will be anchored and you'll be ready to sail into new, perhaps uncharted, waters!

Lifesaver Tips

- Some standards are easy to observe; others are more difficult. For example, it's fairly easy to determine if a student is working well in a group and giving input about sources. On the other hand, observing whether a student is "appreciating" a source can be difficult.

- In some cases, it can be difficult to determine if a student knows each individual standard. Lifesaver 14 includes three critical questions to help determine if students know and understand each of the nine Information Literacy Standards.

- The classroom teacher will often need to assist in answering these questions because the standard may not be demonstrated until the final product is complete.

- Covering the basics of each standard in a library orientation is one way to keep students afloat.

- Standard 1 Example: When a class begins a research project, ask the class to write down keywords that they might use to look up information. As students come in to seek information throughout the year, working with small groups of students on which search sites are best is another strategy to assist students in evaluating information.

- Standard 2 and 3 Example: If a student is making a poster demonstrating his or her understanding of the Holocaust, you won't know until the poster is complete if he or she chose the best, or even accurate, sources.

- Standard 4 Example: A student who has free time comes in and looks up price and ordering information for the new Michael Jordan athletic shoes.

- Standard 5 Example: A student who is reading a play by Shakespeare comes in to search the Internet for other plays by this famous writer.

- Standard 6 Example: The student studying Shakespeare discards a play she found online because it has been translated into modern verse and she prefers Shakespeare's original language.

- Standard 7 Example: A student logs off the computer when he sees there are other students who need the computer and he has time to work on his project tomorrow.

- Standard 8 Examples: Include ethical and unethical use of technology and information in your library orientation. Obviously, a discussion of copyright laws can fit well here. Plagiarism is also a good topic to discuss in this context.

- Standard 9 Example: Students work in a small group to determine which three sources (out of ten) they will share in a speech given to the rest of the class.

Lifesaver Trip 13:
Developing Educational Standards

http://edstandards.org/StSu/Library.html

Does your state have information literacy standards in place? Find out here!

THE STANDARD THREE: THREE CRITICAL QUESTIONS

To Help Students Meet Standards

Standard 1: Assesses information efficiently and effectively

- Does the student know what he or she is looking for?
- Does the student know how to ask for what he or she needs?
- Does the student know three (or more) sources in which he or she can locate the information needed?

Standard 2: Evaluates information critically and competently

- Does the student know whether the information is accurate?
- Does the student know whether the information is based on fact or opinion?
- Does the student know which information to use? To discard?

Standard 3: Uses information effectively and creatively

- Does the student organize his or her information well?
- Does the student demonstrate critical thinking skills and problem solving?
- Does the student know how to add the information to his or her own knowledge base?

Standard 4: Pursues information related to personal interests

- Does the student seek information related to hobbies?
- Does the student access information to career or other personal interests?
- Does the student use and create the best information found?

Standard 5: Appreciates literature and other creative expressions of information

- Does the student have average (or above average) reading ability?
- Does the student show self-motivation and desire to read?
- Does the student acknowledge creativeness in information found and apply information creatively?

Standard 6: Strives for excellence in information seeking and knowledge generation

- Does the student critically look at and judge the content of each source?
- Does the student revise information found independently?
- Does the student improve information located independently?

Standard 7: Recognizes the importance of information to a democratic society

- Does the student gather information from a variety of sources and formats?
- Does the student appreciate information from other cultures?
- Does the student demonstrate knowledge of equal access of information to all?

(Continued)

THE STANDARD THREE (*Continued*)

Standard 8: Practices ethical behavior in regard to information and information technology

- Does the student respect and understand intellectual freedom principles?
- Does the student respect and understand intellectual rights to property?
- Does the student use information technology in a responsible manner?

Standard 9: Participates effectively in groups to pursue and generate information

- Does the student model the use of information seeking to others?
- Does the student share knowledge with others in groups?
- Does the student work with others to evaluate and use information?

Lifesaver Tool 13. The Standard Three

STANDARDS, SMANDARDS! WHY BOTHER?

Even if you know the standards, it's easy to get buried under your obligations and just go for survival! If you're in this boat, Anderson's article titled "Why Are Media Positions Cut? How *Not* to Survive!" (see Lifesaver 5 below) may just be what you need to get your job anchored! Even if you're already teaching great, quality lessons, the evidence is clear that standards are essential for student achievement. Still doubtful? After seeing Lifesaver 14, I think you'll agree that the bottom line is now being *online* with standards.

Lifesaver Tips

- Copy Lifesaver Tool 14 and keep it posted in a location where people will notice it.

- Give a copy to your school principal. Let him or her know you're teaching the standards.

- Put a copy of the Information Literacy Standards in teachers' mailboxes at the beginning of each year. Get them onboard with the standards.

- Include standards information in your library newsletter.

- When team teaching with teachers, insert the standards into the day's lesson.

- Teaching standards to the teachers is just as important as teaching them to the students.

FIVE LIFESAVERS FOR THE "STANDARD" MEDIA SPECIALIST

Manzo, Kathleen Kennedy. "Study Shows Rise in Test Scores Tied to School Library Resources." *Education Week* (March 22, 2000).

http://www.edweek.org/ew/ewstory.cfm?slug=28libe.h19

The Bottom Line:

"Students in schools with appropriate and sufficient library collections and qualified library personnel tend to perform better on standardized tests, especially in reading."

Lance, Keith Curry. "The Impact of School Library Media Centers on Academic Achievement." *School Library Media Quarterly* 23, no. 3 (Spring 1994).

http://www.ala.org/aasl/SLMR/slmr_resources/select_lance.html

The Bottom Line:

"Students at schools with better-funded Library media centers tend to achieve higher average reading scores. . . . Students whose library media specialists played such a role tended to achieve higher average test scores."

Lance, Keith Curry. "Proof of the Power: Quality Library Media Programs Affect Academic Achievement." *Multimedia Schools* (September 2001).

http://www.infotoday.com/MMSchools/sep01/lance.htm

The Bottom Line:

"These studies indicate that students perform better academically where the library media specialist: 1) is part of a planning and teaching team with the classroom; 2) teaches information literacy; and 3) provides one-to-one tutoring for students in need."

"Ten Reasons Why the Internet Is No Substitute for a Library."

http://www.ala.org/alonline/news/10reasons.html

The Bottom Line

Believe it or not, "not everything is on the Internet!" Read this article to discover the other nine enlightening reasons!

Anderson, Mary Alice: "Why Are Media Positions Cut? How Not to Survive!" *Multimedia Schools* (May/June 2002).

http://www.infotoday.com/MMSchools/may02/anderson.htm

The Bottom Line:

"Core library skills are needed, but alone are not enough!"

I WILL "SURVIVE"— INFORMATION LITERACY SKILLS

Now that you know about the Information Literacy Skills, there's one (well, actually six!) things I may have neglected to mention. Do the words "Big 6" sound familiar?

Lifesaver Tips

- What is "The Big 6" anyway?

    The Big 6 is "a systematic approach to information problem-solving." In other words, The Big 6 helps students learn "information literacy for the information age."

- Who came up with The Big 6?

    Michael B. Eisenberg and Robert E. Berkowitz

- What are the six parts of The Big 6?

    1. Task Definition
    2. Information-Seeking Strategies
    3. Location and Access
    4. Use of Information
    5. Synthesis
    6. Evaluation

- Why use The Big 6? (Source: http://www.big6.org/)

    In an online poll, responders preferred The Big 6 for a combination of reasons. Media specialists believed The Big 6 were easy-to-use, easy-to-integrate, and easy-to-teach. The abundance of resources was also a top reason to stick with the six!

Lifesaver Trip 15:
The Big 6 Home Page

http://www.big6.org/

Get free e-newsletters, lessons, and a variety of excellent resources here! I'll give you six great "big" reasons to visit this site.

The Big 6
www.big6.org

1   Task Definition

1.1 Define the information problem

1.2 Identify information needed to complete the task (to solve the information problem)

2   Information-Seeking Strategies

2.1 Determine the range of possible sources (brainstorm)

2.2 Evaluate various possible sources to determine priorities (select the best sources)

3   Location and Access

3.1 Locate sources (intellectually and physically)

3.2 Find information within sources

4   Use of Information

4.1 Engage (e.g., read, hear, view, touch) the information in a source

4.2 Extract relevant information from a source

5   Synthesis

5.1 Organize information from multiple sources

5.2 Present the information

6   Evaluation

6.1 Judge the product (effectiveness)

6.2 Judge the information problem-solving process (efficiency)

Lifesaver Tool 15. The Big 6 Skills

Library Lifesaver 15 is based upon The Big 6 Skills, adapted with permission.
The Big 6™ is copyright ©1987 Michael B. Eisenberg and Robert E. Berkowitz.

Library Lifesaver 16

HEADS UP, 7 UP!

Lifesaver Tips

Library Lifesaver 16 is my adaption of The Big 6. I certainly don't claim that these are better than the original; I just know my own students learn better when things are "spelled out." Not to be outdone by The Big 6, I've named my adaptation "The 7 Up"! Just like with the standards, you'll need a handy chart to help you SURVIVE record keeping. Lifesaver Tool 16A is one you'll need when your students begin to drink up the standards! Lifesaver Tool 16B is your lesson plan lifesaver!

Some Helpful Reminders . . .

* There are nine Information Literacy Standards.

* The Information Literacy Standards are designed as a safety net for teaching library skills.

* The Big 6 are tools to teach those nine Information Literacy Standards.

* Think of the standards as home and the tools as different roads to get there.

* Don't be overwhelmed—chances are, you're already teaching the standards using appropriate tools.

* Now you're just learning the jargon and using checklists to track what you've already been doing.

* The 7 Up is simply my adaptation of The Big 6 to help me survive—use whichever method is most comfortable for you!

Lifesaver Trip 16:
Information Literacy Adventure

http://prwww.ncook.k12.il.us

Use this fun problem-solving activity to teach students valuable information skills. Take students on a Big 6 mountain journey for an exciting skills-based adventure.

LESSON: _____ DATE: _____

SURVIVE the 7 Up! Teaching Information Skills	Completed
S **Study the task** *What is the assignment? What do I need to do?*	
U **Utilize a search strategy** *What are all of my possible sources? Where do I access them?*	
R **Review the sources found** *Do I need all these sources? Which ones can I do without?* *Do I need more?*	
V **Verify that the sources found match the assignment** *Can I do the assignment with what I have? Where do I start?*	
I **Indulge in and information!** *How can I organize the information to best complete* *the assignment?*	
V **View the completed project and prepare to present findings** *Am I ready to present? Is there anything else I still need to do?*	
E **Evaluate and analyze** *What could I do differently/better next time?*	

Lifesaver Tool 16A. Survive the 7 Up!

STANDARDS-BASED LESSON PLAN

Lesson Title:

Standards Targeted	Indicators of Performance	Assessment	Objectives	Strategy/Activities

Lifesaver Tool 16B. Standards-Based Lesson Plan

I'LL BET YOU "CAN" SURVIVE RESEARCH!

If your students are like mine, they need all the organization they can get! This 7 Up Survival Guide (Lifesaver Tool 17) doesn't guarantee students will get the assignment turned in, but at least it's a "step" in the right direction!

Lifesaver Tips

- Before passing out 7 Up handouts, discuss each of the seven steps with students.

- Ask students to show you (in words) what each step "looks like."

- As an extra incentive, I have a drawing for a free 7 Up soda at the end of each class.

- If students are not on task, they are ineligible for the free soda (Believe it or not—this works as well for seniors as it does for second graders!)

- Because the 7 Up Survival Guide can be used for virtually any research assignment, run off lots of copies at the beginning of each year.

- I suggest running off copies in—you guessed it—7 Up Green!

Lifesaver Trip 17:
The Official 7 Up Home Page

http://www.7up.com/

Every year for my 7 Up promotional kickoff, I use petty cash funds to purchase 7 Up T-shirts, temporary tattoos, and other great items. I then hold media center drawings and announce winners over the intercom. It's a fun way to promote the media center and learning at the same time. Beware: high school students "drink up" the "Up Yours" T-shirt, slogan, but younger students need the other T-shirt option.

7 UP RESEARCH SURVIVAL GUIDE

Name: _____ Date: _____

Teacher: _____ Class:_____

Topic Due by:_____

Searching/Information Due by:_____

Project Due by:_____

7 Up STEP ONE:

S Study the task

What is the assignment? Write it down below.

_____

_____

_____

List five steps needed to complete the project:

1.

2.

3.

4.

5.

7 Up STEP TWO:

U Utilize a search strategy

What are four possible sources? Where do I go to access these sources?
Internet, school library, public library, classroom library, teacher . . .

1. *Example: Printed information Internet: www.google.com*

2.

3.

4.

(Continued)

7 Up STEP THREE:

R Review the sources and record information found.

Do I need all sources listed above?

Place a check beside sources you need.

Mark off sources you don't need.

List new sources you find below.

Record notes from information found (Notes can be a list, paragraph, or picture.)

7 Up STEP FOUR:

V Verify that the sources found match the assignment.

Can I do the assignment with what I have? Where do I start? What do I do now?

Evaluate the source of each Internet document found. Is the source credible and reliable?

Ask your teacher or librarian to help you if you are unsure how to verify Internet sites.

7 Up STEP FIVE:

I Indulge and use information!

How can I organize the information to best complete the assignment?

Report

Chart

Poster

PowerPoint Presentation

Other:

7 Up STEP SIX:

V View the completed project and prepare to present findings.

Am I ready to present? Is there anything I still need to do?

Include written source information in your final project. Ask your teacher or librarian to help you with the correct format to cite sources.

7 Up STEP SEVEN:

 Evaluate and analyze results.

Review your graded project. If you don't understand your grade, talk to your teacher.

What could you do differently or better next time?

Lifesaver Tool 17. 7 Up Research Survival Guide

7 UP POSTER ASSIGNMENT: QUENCH THIRST FOR LEARNING INFORMATION SKILLS AND WET APPETITES FOR GREAT BOOKS!

Lifesaver Tips

- Recommended Grade Levels: 6–12

- The amount of details increase with grade level (duh!).

- Award the top three posters a 7 Up prize!

- Assist the classroom teacher in evaluating posters.

- Save the best posters for models during next year's poster assignment.

- For a colorful display, assign students poster boards of different colors.

- Use the caption "Heads Up, 7 Up!" for your window display.

Lifesaver Trip 18: State Book Award Links

http://www.edupaperback.org/lnkaward.html

Link to book awards for every state here! Rather than endanger your "state of mind," bookmark this link of student papers for this assignment!

7 UP POSTER ASSIGNMENT

S **Study the task.** *What is the assignment? What do I need to do?*

☑ Make a "book talk" poster (use standard-size poster board).

Include

☑ Author's full name, date of birth/death, three to five sentences of biographical information, including works published, family information, awards, and so on

☑ Complete title of book

☑ Copyright date and publisher information

☑ Type of book (fiction, nonfiction, story collection)

☑ A "blurb" about the book—don't tell the ending! (Do discuss the most exciting part to make others want to read it.)

☑ Picture of the book and author (feel free to include others for visual appeal!)

☑ Typed list of sources (Works Cited) glued on back of the poster

U **Utilize a search strategy.** *What are possible sources? Where do I access them?*

☑ Internet sites such as Amazon.com and Barnesandnoble.com will include photos of the book and reviews.

☑ Internet search engines (www.google.com) will contain author biographical information.

☑ Print sources: encyclopedias, books, *Something about the Author,* Media Center professional magazines (ask media specialist)

R **Review the sources found.** *Do I need all sources? Which ones don't I need? Do I need more?*

☑ Need more? Have you checked both the school and public library? Ask a librarian!

V **Verify that the sources found match the assignment.** *Do these sources work? Where do I start?*

☑ Write down all source information now. Ask your teacher or librarian for correct format.

I **Indulge and Use Information.**
How can I organize all this information to best complete the assignment?

☑ Exhaust your sources. Dive into your project.

☑ Put together your poster—refer to the above information.

V **View completed project and prepare to present.** *Are you ready? Did you*

☑ review 7 Up Step One to see if any information was overlooked?

☑ clearly write your full name on the poster?

☑ check for spelling and grammatical errors?

☑ use a variety of color and illustrations?

E **Evaluate and analyze the results.** *What could I do differently or better next time?*

Project Grade:_____

Suggestions for improvement:

Lifesaver Tool 18. 7 Up Poster Assignment

"SEA" HOW YOU'RE DOING—A STANDARDS SELF-CHECK

Still not sure about all this standards stuff? Here's a self-check to help you measure how great of a job you're doing! (If it makes you feel better, I "sea" that I have lots of room for improvement!).

Lifesaver Tips

- If you score mostly 1s, you're onboard with the standards!

- If you score mostly 2s, you're setting sail with the standards, but may need to travel more often!

- If you score mostly 3s, you're about to walk the "standard" plank!

Lifesaver Trip 19: Standards Scavenger Hunt

http://www.education-world.com/a_lesson/02/lp261-05.shtml

"SEA" IF YOU'RE MEETING THE STANDARDS

Standard	Often 1	Sometimes 2	Rarely 3
1. I look at the standards before selecting lesson materials.			
2. I choose instructional strategies to meet skills and standards.			
3. I assess what students already know before each lesson.			
4. When necessary, I provide documentation of student learning.			
5. I reteach skills if I feel students have not grasped the concepts.			
6. I use enrichment for students who demonstrate skills and standards.			
7. I modify lessons for students with special needs.			
8. I keep records of classes and their progress on standards.			
9. I know the standards and share information with others.			

Lifesaver Tool 19. "Sea" If You're Meeting the Standards

ARE YOU A MATCH FOR THE STANDARDS?

Ready for a challenge? Here's a little matching game to test your knowledge of the "standard" jargon!

Lifesaver Tips

- For a fun activity at your next teacher meeting or workshop, hand out a copy of this matching game to test your colleagues (and principal!).

- Using "standard" terminology gives you a professional image and adds credibility.

- Share this activity with your media specialist colleagues—it's important—and might even mean job security! (See Lifesaver Tool 13)

Lifesaver Trip 20:
Putting It All Together

http://www.surfline.ne.jp/janetm/big6info.htm

Janet Murray's article "Applying Big 6 Skills, Information Literacy Standards And ISTE NETS to Internet Research" pulls skills, information literacy standards, and even technology standards together in an easy-to-use chart form. It's a lifesaver!

YOUR "STANDARD" VOCABULARY

See if you can supply the correct definition from the right column to the skills listed in the left column.

Skill	Definition
ALIGNMENT	The way instruction is delivered (examples: questioning, discussion)
CURRICULUM	A statement that describes 1) student learning and 2) how that learning will be assessed
CURRICULUM ARTICULATION	Level of performance needed for students to meet each standard
CURRICULUM COORDINATION	How a teacher knows whether a standard has been met; the way students demonstrate they understand the standard
CURRICULUM MAPPING	The knowledge students need for success
STANDARDS	Documenting over time what has been and needs to be taught; making sure all learning gaps are filled
INDICATORS OF PERFORMANCE	Lateral/horizontal flow of focus and curriculum in a school environment
BENCHMARK	When curriculum is focused from one grade to the next or one school to the next
OBJECTIVES	Plan developed for teachers to use in classrooms
STRATEGY	The "match" between the curriculum, the instruction, and tests to be used to assess learners

Lifesaver Tool 20. Your "Standard" Vocabulary

Answer Key to Your "Standard" Vocabulary

The skills apply to the definitions in this order:

- Strategy: The way instruction is delivered (examples: questioning, discussion)

- Objectives: A statement that describes 1) student learning and 2) how that learning will be assessed

- Benchmark: Level of performance needed for students to meet each standard

- Indicators of Performance: How a teacher knows whether a standard has been met; the way students demonstrate they understand the standard

- Standards: The knowledge students need for success

- Curriculum Mapping: Documenting over time what has been and needs to be taught; making sure all learning gaps are filled

- Curriculum Coordination: Lateral/horizontal flow of focus and curriculum in a school environment

- Curriculum Articulation: When curriculum is focused from one grade to the next or one school to the next

- Curriculum: Plan developed for teachers to use in classrooms

- Alignment: The "match" between the curriculum, the instruction, and tests to be used to assess learners

SS 3

DIVE UNDER COVER: LESSONS TO IMPROVE READING MOTIVATION

Lifesaver 21

READING IS A LIFESAVER!

This lifesaver really is a lifesaver for those in need. The fun activity motivates students to read and raises money for charity. What more could you want?

Lifesaver Tips

- Recommended Grade Level: K–8

- Recommended Time: One Grading Period

- Students complete a lifesaver each time they finish a book.

- For manageability purposes, this activity should be done in homeroom.

- Connect lifesavers together to make a lifesaver "rope."

- Start lifesaver rope at each classroom door (classrooms can work together, if desired).

- When the lifesaver rope reaches the office door, the principal performs a funny task (for example: principal dresses in a bear costume, gets a pie in the face, shaves his—or her!—head).

- Have a penny drive in homeroom while doing this activity.

- Post "Reading is a Lifesaver" slogan on coffee cans to collect pennies.

- The principal, the Parent-Teacher Organization, or parents can donate a penny for each lifesaver ring posted to earn even more money.

- Donate money to the American Red Cross or another worthy charity.

- When a class' lifesaver rope reaches the office, the fundraiser is over and that class gets lifesaver candy treats. (Don't forget to make allowances for those classrooms closer to the office!)

- Another option is to have a pool party at the conclusion of this motivational reading activity (it's helpful if your school has a pool!).

- To form the lifesaver rope, make a small, straight cut on the lifesaver and then insert a lifesaver ring to form a chain.

Lifesaver Trip 21:
American Red Cross Home Page

http://www.redcross.org/donate/donate.html

Find out how to donate online, locate volunteer activities, and use the zip code locater to find your local chapter. Discover how your school can be a lifesaver to your community!

Lifesaver Tool 21. Reading Is a Lifesaver!

DEAR DIARY, THIS BOOK IS GREAT!

Nancy Witty, my mentor and friend, always has the "write" idea. This year she came up with the idea of tying in reading journals to library class. Her school, like many others across the country, is focusing on improving writing skills as a part of their school improvement plan, and Nancy knew she wanted to take part. Her response to the challenge to improve writing and reading scores was to create Lifesaver Tool 22. You'll probably want to start using it yourself "write" now!

Lifesaver Tips

- Reproduce a journal for each student (Grades 2 and up) at the beginning of the year.

- Primary students begin their journals second semester.

- Journals cost about $40.00—just enough to cover brightly colored paper.

- Nancy uses journals at least once per six weeks—you can use them as much (or as little) as you want.

- Students can keep track of books they have read.

- Students may choose to make comments on books they especially liked—or disliked.

- Nancy allows her students to write on any page they want in the journal.

- Nancy's students can write about anything they want, as long as it pertains to reading or books.

- Her journal pages are divided into the following sections:

    – Books I've Read
    – Books I Want to Read
    – Favorite Characters
    – Favorite Lines

The rest of the journal is blank, allowing students to make their own headings.

- The back of the journal lets the student decide whether they wish to share it with others.

- Nancy uses the "No Talk, No Walk" rule—in other words, all students write without distractions for at least fifteen minutes.

- To get her students writing, Nancy often takes the advice of her mentor, Ruth Ayres, when deciding which read-aloud to choose: "If it's gory, they'll love it!" Twenty eight years later, the strategy still works!

Nancy Witty

Lifesaver Trip 22:
Writing Topics

http://www.thewritesource.com/topics.htm

Start your students off on the "write" foot by giving them lists of possible topics when they're stuck. Topics for every grade level, as well as other writing resources, can be found here.

MY READING JOURNAL!!!

NAME:

TEACHER:

YES, TAKE A LOOK!

PRIVATE! FOR MY EYES ONLY! :-(

Lifesaver Tool 22. Reading Journal

STUDENTS WHO READ ARE ON THE BALL!

This lifesaver has as many adaptations as a ball has bounces! It can easily work with all grade levels. Unlike some of the other reading motivational strategies, this one works well at the high school level. Even the seniors have a ball (literally!) with this one!

Lifesaver Tips

- Recommended Grade Levels: K–12

- Recommended Time: Yearlong Activity

- Every time a student reads a book, his or her "ball" (Lifesaver Tool 23) is put in the basket.

- Each ball has the name of the student and the title of the book he or she read.

- The basket is kept in a secure location so that only teachers may place balls in basket.

- Start the activity at the beginning of the year.

- "Aim" for the culminating activity at the end of the year.

- At the end of the year (or when your school chooses), the principal "rebounds" balls from the basket to form a student versus faculty basketball team.

- Students whose names are drawn may either choose to play in the tournament or choose players to represent them (another student or a parent!) in the big game.

- Obviously, faculty members will need to be drafted!

- Optional: Faculty versus student cheerleaders definitely scores points for fun!

- The game can be held at lunch (if it's easier) or, better yet, at a pep session.

- Distribute press releases to local media to notify them of the game and the reading activity that has taken place all year.

- This activity can turn into a nice fundraiser if the game is held in the evening and a small admission fee is charged.

- Any money that "dribbles" in could be used to purchase new library books!

Lifesaver Trip 23:
Read to Achieve

http://www.wnba.com/community/readtoachieve_020508.html

See how well your students score with this motivational reading program sponsored by the Women's National Basketball Association!

READING IS A BALL!

TITLE:_____

NAME:_____ GRADE:_____

Lifesaver Tool 23. Reading Is a Ball!

Image © 2002-2003 www.clipart.com

GET OUT OF THE DOGHOUSE—READ!

You'll never bark up the wrong tree with this fun, motivational reading activity!

Lifesaver Tips

- Recommended Grade Levels: K–8

- Recommended Time: One Grading Period

- Throw students a bone each time they read a book.

- A "purr-fect" idea is to ask students to read nonfiction animal books during this activity.

- Post the bones (Lifesaver Tool 24) in the hallway.

- Play the song "Who Let the Dawgs Out?" by the BaHa Men each time you start sustained silent reading during this month.

- Allow students to bring in stuffed animals (preferably dogs) on Fridays.

- When students earn ten bones, they receive a dog tag necklace.

- Ask your Parent-Teacher Organization to help take a bite out of the dog tag costs.

- Use this reading activity to raise awareness for your local humane shelter.

- Ask student groups to make posters that includes the humane shelter number and address.

- Local humane shelters may be willing to sponsor a poster contest and give away a free pet (don't forget to get parent permission—their bark might not be worse than their bite!)

Lifesaver Trip 24

http://www.orientaltradingcompany.com/

Purchase dog tags here! Aluminum, 60s-style dog tag necklaces are only $2.49/dozen. Metallic, neon-colored dog tag necklaces are only $2.95/dozen.

After this fun activity, students will see that reading isn't "ruff" after all!

No Bones about It—Reading Is Fun!

Title: _____

Name: _____ Grade: _____

Image © 2002-2003 www.clipart.com

Lifesaver Tool 24. No Bones about It—Reading Is Fun!

READ AROUND THE CLOCK!

Want to get kids really excited about reading? Have a dance! There's really only "two steps" to this activity—get pledges and get reading!

Lifesaver Tips

- Recommended Grade Levels: 6–12

- Recommended Time: One Grading Period

- By earning pledges (see Pledge Sheet: Lifesaver Tool 25), this activity pays for itself.

- Students can earn pledges by the number of pages read or number of hours read.

- The pledges earned pay for dance decorations, a DJ, and snacks.

- Extra money can be used to pay for—what else—music and dance books!

- Students can earn free admission to the dance by participating in the reading activity.

- Students who choose not to read can purchase a dance ticket.

Lifesaver Trip 25:
Stumps—America's Prom and Party Favorite

http://www.stumpsprom.com/

Don't be stumped about planning and decorating ideas for the big dance. This site is your one-stop shopping place for parties. Your students may even choose to join the teen advisory board to assist with party issues nationwide. Read all about it on the Web site!

READ AROUND THE CLOCK PLEDGE FORM

Pledge Maker Name (Last, First)	Phone Number	Address	Amount Pledged	Paid

Lifesaver Tool 25. Read around the Clock Pledge Form

GOD BLESS THE USA—READ!

      This motivational reading activity will get your students in the right "state" of mind! This lifesaver is aimed at students who are "graduating" and going to another school the next year. It's a reading celebration and graduation party all in one!

Lifesaver Tips

- Recommended Grade Levels: Grades 5–8

- Recommended Time: Yearlong Activity

- Assign each student a state book to start the activity.

- After a quick comprehension check in which the student "states" key facts, the teacher then initials the state.

- The student then colors in the corresponding state on the map (Lifesaver Tool 26).

- The student chooses a book on a different state to read.

- As each book is read, the corresponding state gets colored in until the entire map is filled.

- At the end of the year, students who have successfully filled in every state on the map (or a predetermined amount) get to go on the class trip.

- This activity is aimed at nonfiction reading, therefore the student's book of choice may include library books, encyclopedias, textbooks, Internet sites, or other librarian and teacher approved resources.

- Because many schools already have end-of-the-year trips for graduating students, this activity can be a nice tie-in for a fun-filled bus trip to another state!

Note: This activity coordinates nicely with Library Lifesaver 44 in *100 Library Lifesavers*, p. 134).

Lifesaver Trip 26:
United States Geography Web Site

http://members.aol.com/bowermanb/US.html

From do-it-yourself color-coded state maps to dumb laws, this site has it all mapped out!

The United States

Lifesaver Tool 26. The Fifty States

For map key, go to http://www.clickandlearn.com/giffiles/cluesUSA.gif.

READING IS THE TICKET!

This activity gives a whole new meaning to your typical "Reader's Theatre!"

Lifesaver Tips

- Recommended Grade Level: K–12

- Recommended Time: Summer Reading Promotion

- This reading activity ties in with summer reading incentives at the public library.

- This activity also involves community partnerships with the local cinema.

- Obviously, you will want to work with members of the public library staff to make sure they're on the same "page." If you don't already work closely with them, they may need to "butter up" the staff to get their support.

- Contact the manager of a local cinema well in advance and see if he or she is willing to host a "Reading Is the Ticket" night in which students can get in free for participating in the summer reading program.

- Each time students read a book, they fill out a "ticket" (Library Lifesaver 27).

- Parents sign the ticket to ensure the student did, in fact, read the book.

- The ticket is placed in a jar at the public library.

- At the end of the designated time, the public librarian or a staff member pulls out the tickets.

- If students submit five tickets (i.e., they have read 5 books), they get into the local movie theater free on the designated "Reading Is the Ticket" night.

- Take pictures during the event and submit them to the local newspaper—it's great publicity for the school, the public library, and the movie theater!

- If students turn in ten or more tickets, they get free popcorn to enjoy during the movie as well.

   Note: This activity could be adapted to the school year and students could read at home.

Lifesaver Trip 27:
Moviefone Online—It's Just the Ticket!

http://www.moviefone.com/

   If a movie theater hasn't agreed to provide tickets to your students, purchase movie tickets online at this Web site so you don't have to wait in line!

READING IS THE TICKET!

NAME_____

AGE_____ GRADE_____ PHONE_____

TITLE OF BOOK
READ_____

PARENT/LIBRARIAN
SIGNATURE_____

NAME_____

AGE_____ GRADE_____ PHONE_____

TITLE OF BOOK
READ_____

PARENT/LIBRARIAN
SIGNATURE_____

NAME_____

AGE_____ GRADE_____ PHONE_____

TITLE OF BOOK
READ_____

PARENT/LIBRARIAN
SIGNATURE_____

Lifesaver Tool 27. Reading Is the Ticket!

READING IS "WRITE"

Author visits certainly aren't new to any librarian. Finding out about current author information and pricing, however, can be a little tricky! This lifesaver can help you get the "write" idea when planning your next author extravaganza.

Lifesaver Tips:
Planning Potential Costs for Author Visits

- Travel (airfare or fuel costs)
- Lodging
- Speaking Fee
- Meals
- Book Purchases
- Refreshments
- Catering
- Programs
- Setup Fees
- Publicity

Lifesaver Trip 28:
Author and Illustrator Visits

http://www.tonibuzzeo.com/

This awesome site offers tips to ensure a terrific author visit, e-mail addresses to contact authors online, and a wealth of other lifesavers! Don't miss it!

AUTHOR VISIT CONTRACT

To:

From:

Date:

Our library is pleased to invite you to speak to our students in Grades _____ to _____. The date(s) we have selected are listed below:

_____

_____

The tentative schedule is as follows:

_____

_____

You will meet with _____classes/students/groups for approximately _____ minutes each. Lunch will/will not be provided. An author book signing will/will not be arranged during your scheduled visit.

A check in the amount of $_____ is enclosed/will be provided to you during your visit. This amount does/does not include air and/or ground travel expenses, lodging and meals.

Please sign this contract and return a copy to me.

We look forward to your visit! Thank you for your commitment to our school and community.

Signed _____
              Library Media Specialist Date:

_____
              Principal Date:

_____
              Author Date:

Lifesaver Tool 28. Author Visit Contract

THE SLICE IS "WRITE!"

Like it or not, nothing motivates my students to read more than food. Any food will usually do, but pizza is the "supreme" motivator!

Lifesaver Tips

- Recommended Grade Levels: K–8

- Recommended Time: One Semester

- Ask your local pizza parlor to donate pizza boxes. Some businesses will donate the boxes free for the extra publicity; others may charge a small fee.

- Distribute pizza boxes to participating students. Students decorate outside of the pizza boxes with their names and personal characteristics (i.e., photos of family and friends, hobbies, favorites—songs, movies, etc.).

- On the inside of the box, students decorate each "slice" (Lifesaver Tool 29) with details from a book they have read. Students should include title, author, character(s), setting(s), and conflict(s). Use the back of the slice if more room is needed. If so, just tape or glue only the top of the "crust" so both sides can be viewed.

- Each slice represents a different book. When the "pizza" is made (approximately eight slices), the activity is finished.

- The class with the most completed pizza boxes by a designated date wins a pizza party. Businesses may even donate pizzas if you don't have enough "dough!"

Lifesaver Trip 29:
Pizza Hut's Book It Program

http://www.bookitprogram.com/

I was pleasantly surprised by the new and improved Book It Program. The program has received a facelift and I think kids will definitely "eat it up!"

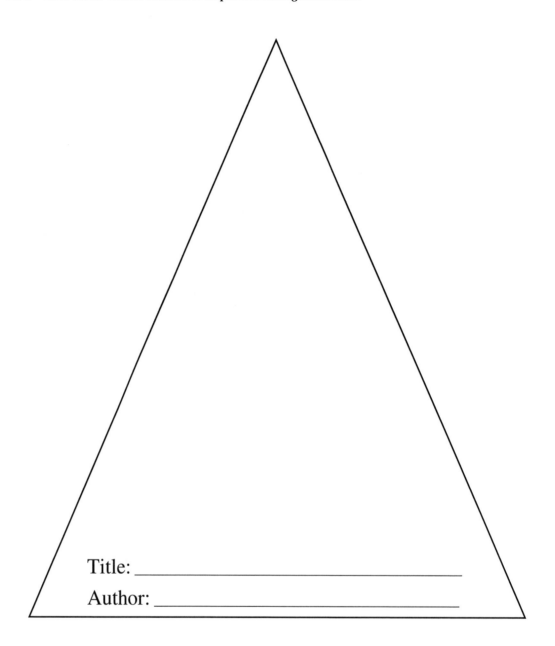

Title: _____

Author: _____

The Slice Is Right!

Lifesaver Tool 29. The Slice Is Right!

MAKE READING COUNT!

If you don't already use a computerized reading tool, try making your time "count" by joining Scholastic Reading Counts. This program contains thousands of computer quizzes that tie in with any grade level or curriculum. The program keeps track of student points, level, and books read, among other key features. A plethora of reports are available at the touch of a key. It's a lifesaver you can count on.

(Author's Note: I don't necessarily endorse this program over the Accelerated Reader program; this is simply the program I know and trust!)

Lifesaver Tips

- Recommended Grades: K–12

- Recommended Time: Entire School Year

- The strength of the Scholastic Reading Counts (SRC) program is its adaptability—it works as well with elementary students as it does with college-bound seniors.

- At high grade levels, many teachers use the accumulated SRC points for a mandatory grade; other teachers use the points as extra credit at the end of each grading period.

- For information, log on to the Web site at http://www.readingcounts.com.

- Make contact by phone at 1-877-COUNTS-1.

- The "My Library" feature matches the books your library has with the computer quizzes you need—what a valuable timesaver!

- The Scholastic Reading Inventory (SRI) option allows you (or the classroom teacher) to assess each student's reading level and make personalized reading recommendations.

- Personalized professional development training is available—or newbies can attend a one-day workshop offered in several cities throughout the country.

Lifesaver Trip 30:
Scholastic Reading Counts Home Page

http://www.readingcounts.com/

Make your time count and order quizzes and reading incentives online!

SIX REASONS TO MAKE READING COUNT AT YOUR SCHOOL

1. The program is easy to implement. You don't even have to buy new books. The program works with the books you already own. You just need to purchase quizzes to install on one—or all—computers.

2. Reading improvement is mandatory with today's high-stakes testing—and your library can play an integral part!

3. Self-selected reading is the key to creating lifelong readers.

4. Motivation in terms of points and incentives can be a boost for reluctant or struggling readers.

5. Reading comprehension improves with practice.

6. The program individualizes reading instruction by providing a list based on each student's personal interests and abilities.

Lifesaver Tool 30. Six Reasons to Make Reading Count at Your School

SS 4

KEEP AFLOAT: GREAT LIBRARY MANAGEMENT TIPS

AVOIDING THE "P" WORD—PLAGIARISM

Did you know that most college-bound students have admitted to cheating, and even more students believe cheaters don't get caught? Whether or not students intentionally cheat (I prefer to believe they don't do it purposefully), turnitin.com can help. Students in today's "techie" generation, who may simply know their way around the computer a little too well and don't always fully understand ramifications of the all-too-easy cut and paste features, may never have to learn the "P" word!

Lifesaver Tips:
Turn in Papers to Turn Off Plagiarism

• What Is Turnitin.com?

   Turnitin.com is the newest way to help prevent students from plagiarizing.

• How Does Turnitin.com Work?

   Turnitin.com works in two ways. One way is for teachers to submit suspicious papers to turnitin.com for review. The second way is for students to submit their own papers to turnitin.com and see if any parts are plagiarized. The way it works is simple. Papers are submitted to turnitin.com via cut and paste or retyped. Turnitin.com receives papers and checks them against the Internet for any "matches." After a thorough check, reports are returned to teachers (or students) within 24 hours. The color-coded report shows Internet matches and gives a percentage of what part (if any) of the paper is plagiarized. In the past, a teacher may have suspected plagiarism but didn't have the tools, time, or resources to investigate. This has changed with turnitin.com.

• How Much Does Turnitin.com Cost?

   There are different rates available—for teachers, schools, and individuals. When I first joined, I paid $40 per year. I believe the charge is now $100, but I find the cost well worth it. Simply making students aware that we are members of turnitin.com has made students more aware of how they use resources.

Lifesaver Trip 31:
Turnitin.com Home Page

http://www.turnitin.com/

Turn on your computer and go to this great site for user testimonies, pricing, and all the information you need to get your students to turn over a new leaf.

Eight Ways Turnitin.com Helps Prevent Plagiarism

 Tell your students about turnitin.com.

 Use student papers as examples to show them how turnitin.com works.

 Research ways to cite sources and practice, practice, practice!

 Never let students use a source without citing it!

 Instill a sense of honesty in your students by teaching technology ethics.

 Teach students how to submit their own papers to turnitin.com.

 Investigate cases of student plagiarism on the Internet. Raise awareness!

 Note how many cases of plagiarism are uncovered each year.

Lifesaver Tool 31. Eight Ways Turnitin.com Helps

Library Lifesaver 32

TOO MANY BOOKS, TOO LITTLE TIME

"Too Many Books, Too Little Time" is one of my all-time favorite quotes and one—I'm sure—to which we can all relate. This lifesaver wheel (Library Lifesaver 32) helps you keep track of where your time is being spent.

Lifesaver Tips

- You will never get more time in a day—it's how you use time that matters!

- Don't try to accomplish too much in one day.

- Make a new task list every day.

- Prioritize tasks from one to ten (no more than five is ideal).

- Don't waste time waiting on others.

- If you must wait, have something else to do (e.g., review your calendar, make phone calls, read a spiritual book).

- Buy bulk in items you regularly use—you won't have to waste time going to the store!

- Stock up on two to three months worth of frozen food—you'll save valuable supermarket time.

- Take naps to refresh and revitalize.

- Turn off the cell phone when you're trying to accomplish big tasks. Get rid of any unnecessary interruptions.

- Buy all mix-and-match clothes (e.g., khaki goes with everything!) to save time trying to find something to wear.

- Say No. (I'm still trying to learn this one!)

- Reward yourself when you do say no to reinforce this important habit.

Lifesaver Trip 32:
Beat the Clock—Lessons in Time Management for Middle School Students

http://thechalkboard.com/Corporations/DayRunner/lessons/

Lifesaver lesson plans to teach middle school students important time management skills. Time Out! Lessons are easily adapted to other grades as well!

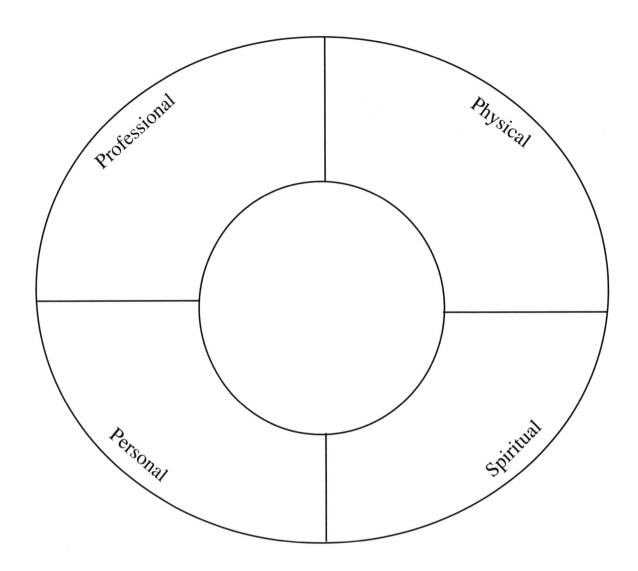

Directions: Rank your progress (on a scale of 1–10) daily in each of the four areas. Monitor where you need to adjust your time to create a better balance. Awareness is a lifesaver!

Lifesaver Tool 32. Beat the Clock

ORGANIZATION—IT'S IN THE PALM OF YOUR HAND!

Palm Pilots (also called PDAs—personal digital assistants) can put organizational strategies at your fingertips—literally!

Lifesaver Tips

- If at all possible, purchase your Palm with color—it's much more user-friendly!

- Never go more than two weeks without synching your Palm and desktop computer—you can lose all your information (I've learned this the hard way!)

- If you're addicted to a paper calendar, print your Palm calendar frequently to supplement your handheld.

- Use the Franklin leather binder and planner organizer if you're still not ready to let go of your traditional calendar.

- Purchase the optional portable keyboard—it's great for taking notes at meetings or writing your memoirs!

- If you don't normally wear pockets, add a purse strap to your PDA (Personal Digital Assistant) case to make your own Palm Purse—wear it at all times (especially at work) for maximum organization. This strategy is much handier than digging through a purse that might not be with you when you need it.

- Practice, practice, practice writing the graffiti—the specialized handwriting used to write on your PDA (see Lifesaver Tool 33 for more on this).

- Purchase the optional $9.95 Lost and Found feature at www.returnme.com. The peace of mind is well worth the ten bucks. This small fee will pay for the safe return of your Palm if it is lost.

- Tired of trying to remember all those passwords, usernames, account numbers, and important dates? The MobileSafe Account Manager handles it all for you for $14.99 (www.handmark.com/products/mobileam).

- Read *How to Do Everything with Your Palm Handheld* by Dave Johnson and Rick Broida ($17.49 at amazon.com).

- Head to NearlyMobile—The Only Site Dedicated to the New Palm User to find the top ten most common newbie problems (www.nearlymobile.com).

- Play the Graffiti Giraffe game often to brush up on your Palm writing skills. You don't want to stick your neck out at an important meeting and be unable to enter important data!

Lifesaver Trip 33: AvantGo.com Home Page

http://www.avantgo.com/

A free Web-based interactive service for handheld devices. Select news, weather, financial travel, sports, entertainment, and other valuable conveniently adapted to the Palm screen size. Let's go!

GRAFFITI WRITING TIPS AND TRICKS

Edgar's Graffiti Tricks Page
http://www.antioch.com.sg/edgar/graffiti.html
This site offers "graffiti gripes" and graffiti shortcuts to turn your graffiti into writing art.

Palm Professor: Graffiti Matters
http://maccentral.macworld.com/news/
0010/10.professor.shtml
Larry Becker's article offers five main "rules" to help you write better, quicker graffiti.

Be a Palm Pro
http://www.cnn.com/2000/TECH/
computing/05/24/being.palm.pro.idg/
Arthur Manzi's article provides Graffiti
Even veteran palm users can bite into the "shortcuts" in his bag of tricks.

Lifesaver Tool 33. Graffiti Writing Tips and Tricks

ROLL OVER PAPERWORK HASSLES!

Between the fax machine, memos, snail mail, and e-mail, paperwork can easily take over our lives. This lifesaver can help you manage mail before you go down with the ship.

Lifesaver Tips

- Purchase an inexpensive rolling cart with three baskets from an office supply store (LTD Commodities; 1-847-295-5532 has an office organizer cart for only $14.95).

- For a more heavy-duty option, purchase Gaiam's sturdy, three-basket cart with large rubber wheels (www.gaiam.com). Because the cart does double duty—it can also be used for recycling—you may want to purchase two ($58 each).

- Label the top (high priority) basket: "TO DO NOW."

- Label the middle (medium/average priority) basket: "TO DO LATER."

- Label the bottom (low priority) basket: "TO FILE."

- Begin by stacking mail into categories (e.g., magazines, catalogs, letters, packages, etc.).

- For items that simply need to be filed for later use, use Post-it notes to mark down where to file the items. This saves time later and can be delegated to a student helper for filing.

- Quickly scan all items. Don't read items in their entirety at this time—especially if you will discard them later.

- Don't pile up mail to read when you have more time—you'll never have more time. Deal with it now, not later.

- If in doubt, throw it away! The rule is never to touch a piece of paper twice!

- Note: If it's possible to delegate this simple sorting task to a library assistant or college intern, do so! Even a student assistant can handle making piles and organizing—then you can do the hard part!

- Remove your name from unwanted mailing lists at www.the-dma.org.

- If you are continually getting mail or catalogs from an unwanted company, contact them and request to be taken off their mailing list. It's a hassle, but this time-saving strategy helps manage the paper clutter.

- Give each all library staff members a mailbox. If an item requires their attention, place it in their box. By not interrupting each other (unless it's something for which one needs an immediate answer, of course), their time (and yours) will be saved.

Lifesaver Trip 34: Get Organized Now!

http://www.getorganizednow.com/

Surf to this lifesaver Web site offering lots of helpful advice on organizing your life. You can even get a free Get Organized kit featuring more than fifty tips and lifesaving strategies! Wow!

ROLL OVER PAPERWORK HASSLES!

R READ AND REVIEW
Immediately open mail, read and review it, and act on it. Does it need to be put in the rolling bin or the waste bin?

O OUT
Throw out anything you don't absolutely need.

L LOOK for and act on items that need immediate attention. If a task only takes a minute, do it and be done with it. If a task requires more time, put it in the top basket.

L LEAVE it.
If it's something you want to save but that doesn't require immediate attention, put it in the file basket and go.

O ONLY handle an item once, if possible.

V VOID your name from unwanted mailing lists.

E ENLIST others to help—delegate this task if you can.

R READ and RESPOND to important mail immediately.

Lifesaver Tool 34. Roll Over Paperwork Hassles!

YOU'VE GOT MAIL!
E-MAIL LIFESAVERS!

Because of the ease and speed of e-mail, it's easy to get addicted. The more you send, the more you receive, which makes you, in turn, get even more e-mail. It's a vicious cycle; however, these lifesaver tips will help you move on to smoother e-mail waters.

Lifesaver Tips

- Managing e-mail is similar to managing snail mail (refer to Library Lifesaver 34).
- If you receive chain letters, jokes, or other unwanted e-mail, reply immediately and ask to be removed from the mailing list.
- Delete unopened e-mail if you can easily detect (from the subject line) it's junk mail.
- Print out important e-mail and place it in the appropriate mail basket (see above).
- Leave e-mail in your inbox as a reminder to act on it.
- Delete e-mail when you have completed the corresponding task.
- Enter new e-mail addresses in your address book or Palm.
- Limit the time you read and respond to e-mail. For example, you may just open e-mail in the mornings when you arrive at work and in the evenings when you get ready to leave.
- For more e-mail and other organizational strategies, read *KISS Guide to Organizing Your Life* by Donald Wetmore (www.amazon.com @ $13.97). You can "kiss" your e-mail problems goodbye!

Lifesaver Trip 35:
Managing the E-Mail Explosion

http://www.pcworld.com/news/article/0,aid,18324,00.asp

Find more tips to manage e-mail before your head explodes (or your computer with all those pending e-mails!)

E-MAIL TO-DO LIST

#	TO-DO	E-MAIL ADDRESS	COMPLETED
1	*E-mail agenda to librarians for upcoming monthly meeting (example)*	*In Address Book*	

Lifesaver Tool 35. E-mail To-Do List

THE POINT OF NO RETURN—PREVIEW PLAN PROCEDURES

We've all done it: agreed to a book preview plan, and before you know it, your time is up and you're left stuck with books you may not want. This lifesaver helps you return preview books before you reach the point of no return!

Lifesaver Tips

- Only agree to book preview plans that offer unlimited time for review.
- Find out who pays the shipping and handling charges—this includes the charges for returning an unwanted book.
- Discover who will make the arrangements to return the item.
- Ask whether there is an obligation to purchase.
- After you return items without purchasing, take note of whether the sales representative is still cordial and professional.
- Preview no more than twenty books at a time.
- Ask about the library discount—is it negotiable?
- Ask about the return policy for unwanted books.
- Make sure your library is not liable for books damaged upon receipt.

Lifesaver Trip 36: Book a Preview!

http://www.librarybooks.com/

One of the best preview plans I've found, this site includes books from Smart Apple Media, Creative Education, and Thameside Press. Includes an online request form and all advantages in the list above.

BOOK PREVIEW RETURN FORM

Date Received:_____Company:_____

Date Returned:_____ Preview #:_____

Sales Representative:_____ Librarian Initials:_____

_____ I am returning all of the preview books. I do/do not plan to purchase any titles at this time.

_____ I am returning all of the preview books except the ones marked on the enclosed preview invoice.

_____ I need a new invoice with the correct amount of purchase.

_____ Please send another preview box on _____.

_____ Please send no more preview boxes to me until otherwise notified.

_____ Please contact me to discuss this order.

_____ Other comments:

School name:_____

School address:_____

School phone:_____ School fax:_____

Contact person:_____

Lifesaver Tool 36. Book Preview Return Form

DON'T GO OVERBOARD ON OVERDUES!

Whether we like it or not, one thing every library can count on (and count up!) is overdue books. This lifesaver will help you manage those irritating overdues—before you become irritated and "book" out the door.

Lifesaver Tips:
Pam's Hit List – Eight Great Ways to Eliminate Overdues

1 The Payment Plan

If students lose books, allow them to make payments on them. As long as they are making an honest effort, I still allow students to check out books. To make this strategy manageable, only collect payments one morning per week.

2 Who's That Knocking at the Door?

Instead of (or in addition to) sending overdue notices, go to classrooms and visit students with overdues. It's a lot more difficult to ignore a librarian than a little overdue notice!

3 "Wanted"—Missing Books—Dead or Alive!

Post names of students with overdues on a prominent hallway bulletin board. This extra reminder works great even at the high school level. Listing names on morning announcements is also an option—if you have too many to list, just announce five to ten students per day.

☼ 4   One "Fine" Day!

In my library (high school), I charge 25 cents per day for "regular" overdue books and $1 per day for overdue reference books. For my time involved, I refuse to deal with anything less than a quarter per book. This larger fine makes students more aware of when their books are due. For some students, fines don't matter—but at least the extra petty cash lets me buy a few new books! Holding grade cards (and diplomas) until the fine is paid is also a "fine" way to get overdue book returned on time. By the way, if you wait until the end of the year to collect money for lost books, it saves time and interruptions (but I'll take money any time I can get it!).

☼ 5   "Get Out of Jail Free!" Card

If your school allows it, hold a monthly detention for students who repeatedly ignore overdue notices (I use the "three strikes, you're out" rule). If a student brings the book back (or responds in any way), they get out of jail free. Responsibility is the "key!" (Lifesaver Tool 37 is the detention notice.)

☼ 6   Forgive and Forget!

Once each semester, I hold a "forgive and forget" day. If the student returns the book, I forgive all fines—no matter how late the book is! Students get a break, and I get overdue books back. Note: Don't hold "Forgive and Forget" days more than once each semester. High school students quickly figure out the way around the system!

☼ 7   Take Two!

In an informal survey, a two-week checkout time was preferred. The majority of librarians felt the two-week period was long enough to read the book—and short enough to remember to return it.

☼ 8   Calling All Parents!

I admit that I hate this task almost more than any other, but it does work. Even at the high school level, parents respond to calls about lost books. When the parent realizes how much the book costs, they hassle their children relentlessly until they return the overdue items. Many parents even call me back to make sure the book was returned.

Lifesaver Trip 37:
LM_NET

http://www.askeric.org/lm_net/

For other great advice on overdues (and everything else), join LM_NET. If you're not already a member, you're "overdue" for some great professional support!

GET OUT OF JAIL FREE CARD!

Hello! Our records indicate that you have _____ overdue library book(s). Please stop by the library to discuss this matter or plan to serve a detention in the library on _____ at _____ A.M./P.M. Bring this "get out of jail free" card with you when you return the book or speak to the librarian. Thank you!

Name:_____Grade:_____

Date Sent:_____

Librarian's Signature:_____

Lifesaver Tool 37. Get Out of Jail Free Card!

TO FLEX OR NOT TO FLEX—GETTING YOUR LIBRARY IN SHAPE!

If you already have a flexible library schedule, or are planning to move to one, this lifesaver gives you some pros and cons to weigh in when making scheduling decisions.

Lifesaver Tips

- For elementary schools, a combination flex and fixed schedule works well. For example, Grades K–2 might have a fixed schedule to gain important library skills lessons; older students can have a fixed schedule when beginning to research thematic lessons.

- For schools with flexible schedules, you might consider building in a fifteen-minute weekly or biweekly checkout time for classes.

- Consider how you will accomplish the teaching of important library skills when moving to a flexible schedule. Will you teach the skills on as as-needed basis or go with a more comprehensive checklist approach?

- In a flexible schedule, you'll probably team with teachers on a more regular basis. See "Team Up with Teachers" (Library Lifesaver 19, p. 57 in *100 Library Lifesavers*) for tips and a great teaming tool.

- A flexible schedule provides more of an opportunity to work independently with students. The Research Contract (Lifesaver Tool 38) provides an easy way to meet individual research needs.

Lifesaver Trip 38:
Position Statement on Flexible Scheduling

http://www.ala.org/aasl/positions/ps_flexible.html/

Read ALA's position on flexible scheduling to make sure your library is ship shape!

LIBRARY RESEARCH CONTRACT

Research Subject or Topic:

Assignment Due:

For this Project, I plan to

_____ Make a Poster

_____ Design a PowerPoint Presentation

_____ Write a report

_____ Give a speech

_____ Other:

Please highlight below each source you have used (or plan to use) on this project.

- Encyclopedia
- Dictionary
- Atlas
- Almanac
- Books
- Magazines
- Videos
- Interviews
- Textbook
- Vertical Files
- Internet
- Notes from television show/news
- Newspaper
- Other sources I plan to use:_____

I do/do not plan to use public library resources.

Research advice from media specialist:

Teacher comments:

Student comments:

Progress report from media specialist:

Lifesaver Tool 38. Library Research Contract

MEETING MINDERS—TIPS FOR HOSTING SUCCESSFUL MEETINGS

We've all been to meetings that are simply a waste of valuable time. The next time you plan a meeting, plan for success!

Lifesaver Tips

- Send out the Meeting Minder (Lifesaver Tool 39) as soon as the time and date of an upcoming meeting has been established.

- Send out the meeting agenda well in advance so that all attendees can review important items before the meeting date. This saves valuable meeting time.

- Meetings should serve two purposes: solving problems and making decisions. Rehashing old issues and topics of conversation should be avoided.

- Keep additional copies of the agenda for the meeting. People may forget to bring their copies.

- Plan an attention-getting HDA (human development activity) to open the meeting.

- Add humor to the meeting by displaying an appropriate cartoon when people enter the meeting room. This sets a positive tone and creates a safe climate—especially important if "touchy" issues will be discussed.

- Serve food.

- Decorate! People appreciate a simple theme and notice special time and efforts taken to make them comfortable.

- Ask a trustworthy member to take minutes. Type the minutes and distribute promptly a day or two following the meeting.

- Plan for potential conflicts and resolve them by refocusing conversation, summarizing main points, and changing the conversation.

- Keep the meeting on track by taking the focus off the subject conversations.

- Model appropriate meeting behavior. Emphasize the importance of positive behavior and no put-downs.

- Set the next meeting date.

- Monitor the meeting—know when to call a break or wrap up the meeting.

- Set the date for the next meeting.

- Thank attendees for coming. Express appreciation for their having taken the time to attend.

Lifesaver Trip 39:
How to Host Successful Meetings

http://www.effectivemeetings.com/guru

Get personal advice from the Meeting Guru who will help you resolve meeting conflicts and dilemmas, such as how to stop meeting skippers, how to maintain audience attention and how to end meetings effectively.

MEETING MINDER

To:_____ From:_____

Meeting Date:_____ Meeting Time:_____ A.M./P.M.

Meeting Location:_____

Agenda Item(s):

Preparation Needed:

Desired Outcome(s):

Follow-ups:

Next Meeting:_____

Lifesaver Tool 39. Meeting Minder

ASSISTANT ASSISTANCE—LIBRARY SCHEDULING

It's easy for all of us to get caught in a rut and not want to break out of our comfort zones. This lifesaver "assists" in creating a flexible schedule, but this one is for staff, not students!

Lifesaver Tips

- This lifesaver is designed for libraries with a full staff (one or two media specialists and two or more library assistants) but can be adapted to fit the needs of libraries with smaller staffs.

- The basic idea is to change responsibilities of staff members on a regular basis by rotating duties among staff.

- By having all staff (including yourself) work all positions, productivity is higher and, when absences occur, any available staff member can fill in.

- Be positive when presenting this new plan to staff members—especially if they've been around for a while.

- Be flexible in planning. Monitor and adjust as needed until you find what works for you and your media center.

- Revise the Library Scheduling Form (Lifesaver Tool 40) as necessary for your unique staffing needs.

- Obviously, even the best library assistant can't (and shouldn't) perform all the duties of a certified and professional library media specialist. After all, it takes years of education and experience to make the higher-level decisions. When assigning duties, keep this in mind.

Lifesaver Trip 40:
School Library Media Specialist Job Postings

http://www.libraryjobpostings.org/libmedia.htm/

Schedule yourself—or someone you know—into a new job!

LIBRARY SCHEDULE FOR THE WEEK OF _____

Monday	Tuesday	Wednesday	Thursday	Friday	
LMS #1	LMS #2	LA #1	LA #2	Other	**Rotation Area**
					Media Center Office
					Circulation Desk
					Reference Desk
					Floor Duty
					Library Classes

Lifesaver Tool 40. Library Schedule

SS 5

GET BELOW THE
SURFACE—LIBRARY SKILLS
FROM THE GROUND UP

YOUR RESEARCH SEARCH IS OVER!

Are you sure you teach great library research skills, but not so sure you're always meeting the standards? This chapter is more than your "standard" research mumbo jumbo—it ties the research and the standards together with tools to make them work for you.

Lifesaver Tips

Information Literacy Skills Covered

- Standard 1: The student who is information literate accesses information efficiently and effectively.

- Standard 2: The student who is information literate evaluates information critically and competently.

- Standard 3: The student who is information literate uses information accurately and creatively.

Unit Objectives

1. Develops problem-solving and critical thinking skills.
2. Works in cooperative groups effectively to obtain information.
3. Discovers information from a variety of sources.
4. Accesses information effectively.
5. Evaluates information critically and objectively.
6. Uses information in a creative way.
7. Assesses the product achieved through the information-seeking process.

Planning

- Direct Instruction from Library Media Specialist (LMS; 20 percent of unit)

    Note: Direct instruction includes the LMS or teacher orally talking students through the research process (turns on student "light bulbs"). This critical piece should be done every time the LMS gives instruction.

- Guided Research Time (80 percent of unit)

- Feedback provided through student conferences with teacher, LMS, or both

- Use of Graphic Organizer (Lifesaver Tool 41)

Procedures

Students work individually or in small groups to

- Explore potential subjects of research

- Narrow research topics

- Plan their research strategy

- Locate information

- Critically evaluate information

- Develop projects

- Revise and edit final projects

- Present information and findings

- Evaluate research strategy and final product

Possible Projects

- Posters (including illustrations, graphs, and time lines)

- Reports (typed with illustrations or graphics)

- PowerPoint presentations (upper grades)

- Oral presentations

- Video report (upper grades)

Assessment

- Students use a rubric to evaluate the research strategies they used.

- LMS or teacher uses same rubric (Lifesaver Tool 42) to evaluate research demonstrated.

- A student conference is held, an agreement is negotiated, and final scores are given.

- Pre- and posttest—a simple ten-question test (Lifesaver Tool 43) to assess what students know before and after the unit.

- Students keep journals (Lifesaver Tool 44) to document progress throughout the research process.

Lifesaver Trip 41: Internet School Library Media Center (ISLMC)

http://falcon.jmu.edu/~ramseyil/libraries.htm

Lifesavers on topics of selection, cataloging, classification, and library media center management—check it out!

LIFESAVER RING

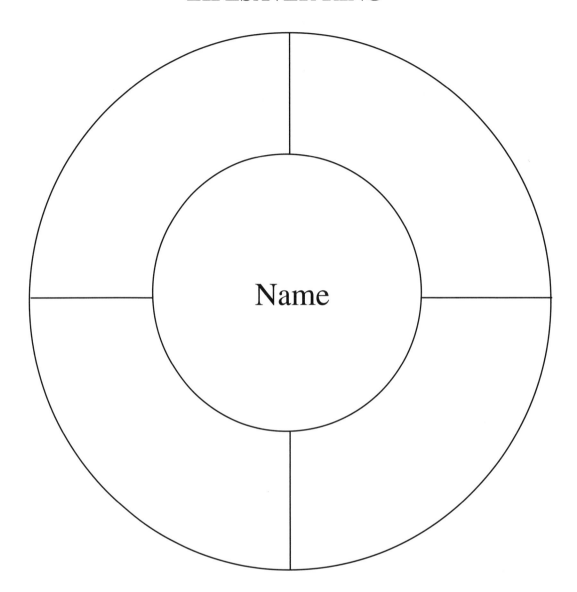

Lifesaver Ring Uses:

1. Students write possible research topics in each of the four lifesaver ring sections. As students decide (individually or in small groups) on a specific topic, that section is colored.

2. Students list four sources in each section of the lifesaver ring.

Lifesaver Tool 41. Lifesaver Ring

"RUBRIC'S CUBE"

This easy research rubric (Lifesaver Tool 42) is an easy way to assess your students' critical thinking skills and help them solve research puzzles.

Lifesaver Tips

- This rubric evaluates the research process—it does not assess the final project.

- This "one size fits all" rubric can be used with most grade levels.

- Why use rubrics?

    1. Rubrics save time—grading is quicker and easier!

    2. No surprises—students know up front how final projects will be evaluated.

    3. Fewer disappointments—more projects meet teacher or library media specialist expectations.

    4. Intentional—ensures standards are met.

    5. Better instruction—matches skills to assessments.

Lifesaver Trip 42:
The Rubricator

http://www.rubrics.com/

Design your own rubrics! This rubric maker software incorporates standards and helps create quality performance assessments quickly and easily. I'm "assessing" it may just be the best $49.95 you'll ever spend!

RUBRIC'S CUBE: RESEARCH SKILLS RUBRIC

Research Skills	Exceeds Standards	Meets Standards	Below Standards (Progressing)	Does Not Meet Standards
Locates *Relevant* Sources				
Uses *Variety* of Sources				
Quality of Sources				
Note Taking/ Organization				
Researches *Independently*				
Time on Task				

Lifesaver Tool 42. Rubric's Cube: Research Skills Rubric

TESTING, TESTING, 1, 2, 3 . . . !

Want a quick, easy way to find out just what your students have learned? Give this quick pretest (Lifesaver Tool 43A and B) to students before and after the research unit. You can look at individual student progress and the classes' progress as a whole. If you put student learning "to the test," they may take researching a little more seriously!

Lifesaver Tips

- For quickest results, use Scantron forms for easy grading.

- Be sure to have sharpened pencils on hand.

- Keep all copies of tests and Scantron forms—you will retest with the same test!

- For security purposes, reorder questions for the retest (if needed).

- Provide classroom teacher with pre- and posttest answers.

- Lifesaver Tool 43A is designed for junior high and high school students. Key: 1) T; 2) F; 3) F; 4) T; 5) F; 6) T; 7) T; 8) F; 9) F; 10) T.

- Lifesaver Tool 43B is designed for elementary school students. Key: 1) F; 2) T; 3) F; 4) T; 5) F; 6) T; 7) T; 8) T; 9) F; 10) T.

Lifesaver Trip 43:
Library Media K–12 Scope and Sequence Overview

http://www.pgcps.pg.k12.md.us/~media1/outcome.html

Get your library skills "in order!"

RESEARCH UNIT PRETEST

Name:_____ Teacher:_____ Grade:_____

"SEARCHING" FOR ANSWERS!

True or False?

When researching, you should use both print and nonprint sources.

You should use ten or more sources when conducting research.

Internet sites are usually reliable, valid sources.

A good way to check the validity of an Internet source is to see who has created the site.

To show a good variety of sources, use three encyclopedias.

It's a good idea to compare different encyclopedias for additional information.

A good search engine to use is www.google.com.

You don't need to take notes if you print out information on all your sources.

There's no need to do research in the library if you have Internet access at home.

You should usually try to locate information yourself before you ask for help.

Lifesaver Tool 43A. Research Unit Pretest

RESEARCH UNIT POSTTEST

Name:_____ Teacher:_____ Grade:_____

True or False?

I should only use the Internet to research information.

I should try to use three or more sources.

I can always believe what the Internet says.

I can usually trust a college or school Internet site.

I will always find the same information in different encyclopedias.

I should start my research with the encyclopedia.

I should start my Internet research at www.google.com.

I should take good notes when I research.

I have a computer so I don't have to use my research time in the library.

I should look for information myself before I ask the librarian for help.

Lifesaver Tool 43B. Research Unit Posttest

RESEARCH THE "WRITE" WAY

This lifesaver teaches students the "write" way to research by keeping journal logs of their progress from start to finish.

Lifesaver Tips

- Don't take time to grade each log.

- Use logs as a qualifier to turn in the project or assign a pass-fail grade to journal entries.

- The journal logs serve as an organizational tool to help students stay on task.

- Scanning logs randomly is a great way to get an "at a glance" measure of student progress.

- The logs encourage higher-level thinking by asking students to write, analyze, and solve problems during the research progress.

Lifesaver Trip 44:
Research Journals

http://www.msdpt.k12.in.us/etspages/pm/imc/Inquiry/journal.htm?1026235344460.

An in-depth look at how research journals can enhance student achievement. Contains links to assessment tools, overheads, and worksheets.

JOURNAL LOG

Date	Research Tasks Accomplished	Problems	Solutions	Questions
M				
T				
W				
Th				
F				

Lifesaver Tool 44. Journal Log

THE LIBRARY—YOUR "SOURCE" FOR RESEARCH!

One of the hardest—and most important—parts of library research is teaching students the correct way to cite sources. This lifesaver provides students with a convenient form to record important source information. In addition, you won't have to sound like a broken "record" telling students what information to record!

Lifesaver Tips

- Distribute this form to students the first day of library research.

- Discuss the importance of filling out all requested information.

- Remind students to record call numbers of books. That way, books can easily be found again if needed.

Lifesaver Trip 45:
Purdue University's OWL (Online Writing Lab) Site

http://owl.english.purdue.edu/handouts/research/

"Who" wants to go to this site? Your students will! The OWL site offers fantastic research paper assistance, including information on how to cite sources.

RESEARCH RECORD

Internet Source:

Title of Web site page:_____
 Usually found at the top of first page

Author (Last, First) if known:_____
 If more than one author, write down all names

http://_____
 Write down full address—usually starts with www.

Date of access:_____ Page numbers:_____.
 Date you looked up information Found at top right-hand corner of i-net page.

Book Source:

Call number: _____
 Found on spine of book and includes numbers and/or letters; tells you where to find the book

Author (Last, First):_____
 If more than one author, write down all names

Title:_____
 Can be found on the book's cover

Publisher:_____
 Can be found on title page

City where published:_____
 Can be found on title page

Page numbers:_____
 Write down all page numbers used

Magazine Source:

Title of article:_____
 Write down all words in title

Author (Last, First):_____
 If more than one author, write down all names

Title of magazine:_____
 Can be found on magazine's cover

Date:_____(Month)_____(Day)_____(Year)
 Can be found on front cover; may not have a day if it is a monthly magazine.

Encyclopedia Source:

Title of encyclopedia article:_____
 In bold print—title is subject you are looking up

Author (Last, First) if known:_____
 Found at the end of the article in small print

Encyclopedia title:_____
 World Book Encyclopedia, Brittanica, Academic American, Encyclopedia Americana, other

Letter(s)_____Volume_____Page #'s_____
 Letter and volume can be found on cover of encyclopedia; Record all pages used.

Other Sources:

Lifesaver Tool 45. Research Record

THE GREAT DEBATE

This lifesaver takes advantage of what some students do best—argue!

Lifesaver Tips

The Great Debate Procedures

- Divide students into two groups.

- Assign students a controversial topic.

- The first group will be in favor of the topic.

- The second group will be against the topic.

- Gather as much information on the topic as possible.

- Remind students that it is important that they know both sides of the topic to debate effectively.

- The three parts of the upcoming debate are opening arguments, rebuttal, and closing arguments.

- Invite the principal to watch the debate.

- Invite the school newspaper or journalism staff to report on the debate.

- During the debate, the rubric is used to judge the debate panelists on their performance.

- The audience members complete the rubric—taking careful notes to back up their answers.

Following is a rough schedule for the Great Debate Project.

- Day One—Gather information on both sides of topic.

- Day Two—Review information and focus on assigned viewpoints in small groups.

- Day Three—Assign students to a debate panel (five per side) or audience (remainder of class) and continue research.

- Day Four—Practice, practice, practice!

- Day Five—The Great Debate!

- Steps for the debate are included in the Great Debate Rubric (Lifesaver Tool 46) on page 138.

Lifesaver Trip 46:
List of Controversial Topics

http://www.uncc.edu/refweb/vrd/hot2.htm

A complete list of controversial topics provided by North Harris College Library with related links. Arguably, a great research site!

THE GREAT DEBATE RUBRIC

	3 Points	2 Points	1 Point
Side 1 Opening arguments	Good preparation Evidence of research Excellent organization	Some preparation Some evidence of research Good organization	Little preparation Little research Poor organization
Side 2 Opening arguments	Good preparation Evidence of research Excellent organization	Some preparation Some evidence of research Good organization	Little preparation Little research Poor organization
Side 1 Rebuttal	Excellent arguments Clear and concise	Good arguments A little unclear Some rambling, off topic	Poor arguments Unclear
Side 2 Rebuttal	Excellent arguments Clear and concise	Good arguments A little unclear Some rambling, off-topic	Poor arguments Unclear
Side 1 Closing arguments	Well rehearsed Great closing	Evidence of practice Good closing	Little practice Poor closing
Side 2 Closing arguments	Well rehearsed Great closing	Evidence of practice Good closing	Little practice Poor closing

Lifesaver Tool 46. The Great Debate Rubric

TAKE TEN!

One of the hardest parts of student research is simply getting started. This lifesaver makes writing ten times easier!

Lifesaver Tips

- This brainstorming activity takes away the hard part of research—getting started.

- After completing the activity, students are less apt to ask, "How should I begin?"

- Turn on an egg timer (or set an alarm) for ten minutes.

- After students have spent a day or two of library research, they "take ten" minutes and write fast and furiously.

- When the timer goes off, the students look over what they have written.

- Highlight in one color parts of the comments that can be used in the research paper.

- Highlight in another color parts of the comments that need more information.

- Review source information to add.

- Divide the ten-minute draft into paragraphs.

Lifesaver Trip 47:
IPL Teenspace: A+ Research and Writing

http://www.ipl.org/div/aplus/

This site gets a "10" for helping students with research and writing.

TAKE TEN!

NAME:_____GRADE:_____

Directions: In the space below, write down as much information as you can about your research topic. Don't worry about grammar or order at this time—just write down as much as you can remember. You will have ten minutes to write. Good luck!

_____
_____
_____
_____
_____
_____
_____
_____
_____
_____
_____
_____
_____
_____
_____
_____
_____
_____
_____
_____
_____
_____
_____
_____

Lifesaver Tool 47. Take Ten!

SET "SAIL" TO GREAT INTERNET SITES!

This lifesaver makes evaluating Internet sources a breeze. Use Lifesaver Tool 48 to help students keep track of the best Internet sites.

Lifesaver Tips

S SCHOLARLY

- Is the site scholarly?
- Does it include references, bibliographies, and footnotes?

A ACCURACY

- Is the site recent? When was the site last updated?
- Is the site accurate?
- Are there noticeable mistakes in spelling or grammar?
- Are there errors in facts?
- Is the site based on facts or opinion?

I INTENDED AUDIENCE

- Is the site too elementary or too advanced?

L LACKING CREDIBILITY

- Is the author's name and background clearly shown?
- Are references available?

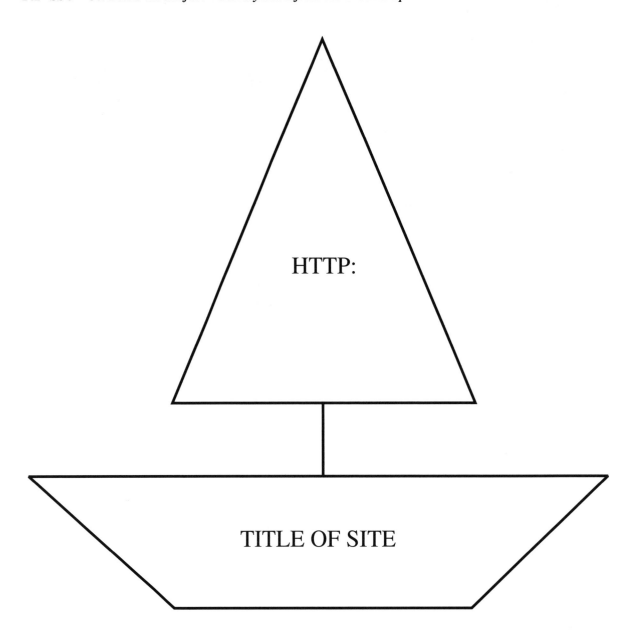

Lifesaver Tool 48. Set Sail for Great Internet Sites!

Out of "Site!"

This lifesaver helps students better understand the Internet as they learn to connect the dots.

Lifesaver Tips

- As students learn to surf the Net, it's important that they understand what the "dots" mean.

- The "dots" are really domain names—extensions on Internet addresses that let users know who sponsors them.

- Hold a quick discussion on why it is important to know who sponsors a Web site (i.e., the commercial .com sites have a much different agenda than the .edu or .org sites—it's big business!)

- Pass out Dots candy for students who earn a perfect score on the matching quiz.

- Use this matching quiz (Lifesaver Tool 49) to find out what students have learned.

Out of Site!

.gov = site hosted by a U.S. government agency

.com = site hosted by a for-profit business

.edu = site hosted by an educational organization (schools, colleges, and universities in the United States)

.org = site hosted by a nonprofit organization

.net = site hosted by a network

.biz = site hosted by a business (newer than .com)

.ac = site hosted by an academic organization (outside the United States)

~ = personal Web page

Lifesaver Trip 49: NetLingo.Com

http://www.netlingo.com/

A great online dictionary of the Internet language. BTW (by the way), there is also a handy chat acronym directory for those of you who (like me) aren't up on all of the latest jargon. EOM (End of Message) SYL (See Ya Later!) Isn't this fun?

OUT OF "SITE!"

Name:_____ Grade:_____

Directions: Match each domain name to the correct definition. If you get them all correct, you'll be out of "site!"

Domain	Definition
.ac	Make up one of your own
.biz	Denotes personal Web page
.com	Site hosted by a nonprofit organization
.edu	Site hosted by a network
.gov	Site hosted by a military organization
.mil	Site hosted by a governmental agency
.net	Site hosted by educational organization or school (in the United States)
.org	Site hosted by a business (sponsored)
~	Site hosted by a business (newer than .com)
.?	Site hosted by an educational organization (outside the United States)

Lifesaver Tool 49. Out of "Site!"

NO ENDINGS, JUST BEGINNINGS!

Unfortunately, I'm often guilty of neglecting this last, but critical, research step. Admittedly, there often just doesn't seem to be enough time, but I truly believe that providing students with an opportunity to evaluate their own work critically will help put an "end" to poor-quality work.

Lifesaver Tips

- Provide a Feedback Form (Lifesaver Tool 50) to students the day the project is due.

- Before students turn in projects, ask them to think about and then respond honestly to all questions.

- If desired, the form could be worth points.

- The form also can be a qualifier (i.e., no form, no grade).

- Students may need time to browse projects before completing the form.

- Question 3 is not intended to generate excuses; it's a way for students to provide personal insights honestly.

- You may want to include a "Process Feedback Form" here as well. If we are teaching information literacy skills, the process is just as important as the product.

Lifesaver Trip 50:
Eduscapes: The Site for Lifelong Learners

http://www.eduscapes.com

Find links to more than two hundred research topics—among dozens of other exciting resources. With a site like this, you may never escape!

PROJECT FEEDBACK FORM

Name:_____ Grade:_____

List three things you like about your project.

List one thing you would change on your project if you had more time.

Do you believe this project is your best effort? Why or why not?

Which of the projects (in our class) do you like best?

What would you change about this project?

Lifesaver Tool 50. Project Feedback Form

SS 6

FLOAT THROUGH PERSONAL AND PROFESSIONAL DEVELOPMENT

X MARKS THE SPOT

One of the biggest areas of professional development today is technology. This life-saver shows where you might want to focus your efforts to take a "byte" out of weak areas.

Lifesaver Tips

- In each of the ten areas, rate your present ability level.

- A score of 3 = good ability (strength area)

- A score of 2 = average ability (comfort area)

- A score of 1 = low ability (area that needs improvement)

- For any weak spots, make a plan on how you will improve in that area. For example, schools often offer after-school technology workshops. Find out what classes are locally available.

Lifesaver Trip 51:
The American Association of School Librarians' Learn to Use the Internet Online Classes

http://www.ala.org/ICONN/onlineco.html

Free online classes to help librarians navigate the Internet and develop technology-related lessons! This site is X-cellent!

TECHNOLOGY SKILLS CHECKLIST

Directions: Place an "X" in the box that accurately measures your current level of proficiency in each of the following areas.

Technology Skill	3	2	1
Use of electronic mail (e-mail)			
Ability to attach a document to an e-mail			
Use of Microsoft Word (or similar word processing program)			
Ability to save and retrieve documents			
Use of Microsoft PowerPoint (or similar presentation program)			
Use of Microsoft Excel (or similar spreadsheet program)			
Use of Internet			
Use of Internet search engines			
Ability to cut and paste documents			
Ability to insert text, tables, and graphics into documents			
Use of CD-ROM programs (downloading, opening, and running)			
Use of computer editing program (such as Microsoft Reviewing)			
Use of Microsoft Publisher (or similar desktop publishing software)			
Use of digital camera			
Use of electronic calendar for planning and organizing schedule			

Lifesaver Tool 51. Technology Skills Checklist

"STRESSING" THE IMPORTANCE OF PROFESSIONAL DEVELOPMENT

The demands of keeping pace with technology and professional development—let alone running an entire library—can seem overwhelming. This lifesaver "stresses" the importance of relaxation.

Lifesaver Tips:
How to Be "Stress Free!"

S SHARE feelings

When you are feeling stressed or anxious, talk to a close colleague. Even if you don't solve the problem, talking can make you feel better.

T TAKE time

Before you start feeling stressed, be proactive and take regular breaks. Walk to get a cold drink or go to the restroom and do some deep breathing. The idea is to take time to feel calm and in control.

R RELAX

Each day I try to carve a few minutes from my busy schedule to relax. For me, the easiest way to relax immediately is to leave the building. I'll run errands, visit the public library, or pick up a drive-through lunch. Even a few minutes away in a different setting relaxes me.

E EXERCISE

This is the most important key I've found to dealing with stress. Even if it's just five minutes per day, I do some type of exercise daily. Even a few minutes boosts my energy level and reduces my stress.

S SUPPORT

> If your stress level feels higher than normal, try talking to your school counselor. Support is critical!

S SET PRIORITIES

> The hardest part of our job is never being able to get caught up. Only by setting priorities and juggling the workload can we prioritize our responsibilities.

F FAITH

> My faith in God is truly the biggest stress reliever—and lifesaver—I've ever found!

R RESPOND differently

> When you find yourself feeling stressed and angry, take a deep breath and respond differently. Remember, the only thing you can control is how you react to a situation!

E ESCAPE

> Whenever you get the opportunity—leave! After all, you've got comp time, and you've earned it!

E EAT right

> Eat a healthy, well-balanced diet and take vitamin supplements. Drink milk and water. (I'm working on the water part—so far I'm not doing too "well!")

Lifesaver Trip 52:
St. Joseph University's Quick Relaxation Tips

http://www.sju.edu/counseling/relaxation.htm

> Find several "quick-release" relaxation techniques here to help relax your mind—and your muscles!

STRESS RELEASE CHECKLIST

Directions: Check the "+" column for areas in which you did well today. Check the "–" box for areas that could use some improvement. Fill out the chart daily, and take note of negative patterns.

			+	–
S	I **shared** feelings with someone today when I was upset.			
T	I had a few minutes of relaxation **time** today at work.			
R	I made myself **relax** after a stressful situation today.			
E	I **exercised** for at least five minutes today!			
S	I made contact with a trusted school counselor for **support.**			
S	I **set priorities** and stuck to them today.			
F	I took a few moments today for **faith.**			
R	I tried to control my **response** to a stressful situation today.			
E	I **escaped** today and left early! ☺			
E	I was careful to **eat** and drink healthily today!			

Lifesaver Tool 52. Stress Release Checklist

FIGHT FAIR—CONFLICT RESOLUTION SKILLS

If you're working with teachers and students (and what school librarian isn't?), it's important to understand how to resolve conflicts. If you're in charge of a library staff, it's even more important. Even with a great staff (like mine!), conflicts occur, and you need to "fight" to resolve them early.

Lifesaver Tips:
Conflict Resolution Network—Twelve Skills Summary

- The Win-Win Approach

  Identify attitude shifts to respect all parties' needs.

- Creative Response

  Transform problems into creative opportunities.

- Empathy

  Develop communication tools to build rapport. Use listening to clarify understanding.

- Appropriate Assertiveness

  Apply strategies to attack the problem, not the person.

- Cooperative Power

  Eliminate "power over" to build "power with" others.

- Managing Emotions

  Express fear, anger, hurt, and frustration wisely to effect change.

- Willingness to Resolve

  Recognize personal issues that cloud the picture.

- Map the Conflict

  Define the issues needed to chart common needs and concerns.

- Development of Options

  Design creative solutions together.

- Introduction to Negotiation

  Plan and apply effective strategies to reach agreement.

- Introduction to Mediation

  Help conflicting parties to move toward solutions.

- Broaden Perspectives

  Evaluate the problem in a broader context.

Lifesaver Trip 53:
The Conflict Resolution Network

http://www.crnhq.org/twelveskills.html

"Resolve" to visit this page for more detailed information on the twelve skills. You can also contact them at P.O. Box 1016 Chatswood, 2057 NSW Australia; Telephone: +61 2 9419-8500; Fax: +61 2 9413-1148; E-mail: crn@crnhq.org

KEYS TO CONFLICT RESOLUTION

C Calm

Remain calm and remember your true desire to work things out.

O Open Your Mind

Be open-minded and listen to all sides—even (and especially) if you don't agree.

N Needs

Recognize the needs of the other parties involved.

F Fairness

Be fair—listen and consider a compromise.

L Listen

Really hear what the other person is saying.

I Itemize

Make a list of all possibilities and brainstorm a list of compromises.

C Consider a Negotiator

If you can't reach a compromise, find an objective third party to help.

T Treat Others with Respect

After the conflict, don't hold a grudge! Be friendly and professional.

Lifesaver Tool 53. Keys to Conflict Resolution

BRAINSTORMING— LIGHTNING-FAST IDEAS

Have you ever had to write a grant, memo, or proposal and just couldn't get started? If you have the time to wait and let the ideas come to you, that's great! Unfortunately, time may not always be on your side. The next time writer's block threatens, try brainstorming.

Lifesaver Tips

- Three types of brainstorming: listing, free-association thinking, clustering.

- Before you begin to brainstorm, set a timer for five minutes.

- The purpose of the timer is to force out thoughts.

- Write furiously, and don't stop before the timer ends.

- Don't judge or analyze thoughts as you jot them down—anything goes!

- Don't worry about spelling or grammar as you write down your thoughts.

Lifesaver Trip 54: Inspiration Home Page

http://www.inspiration.com

Get a little inspiration from this computer software that's great for clustering and webbing. No doubt you'll "brainstorm" other great uses!

BRAINSTORMING LIFESAVER

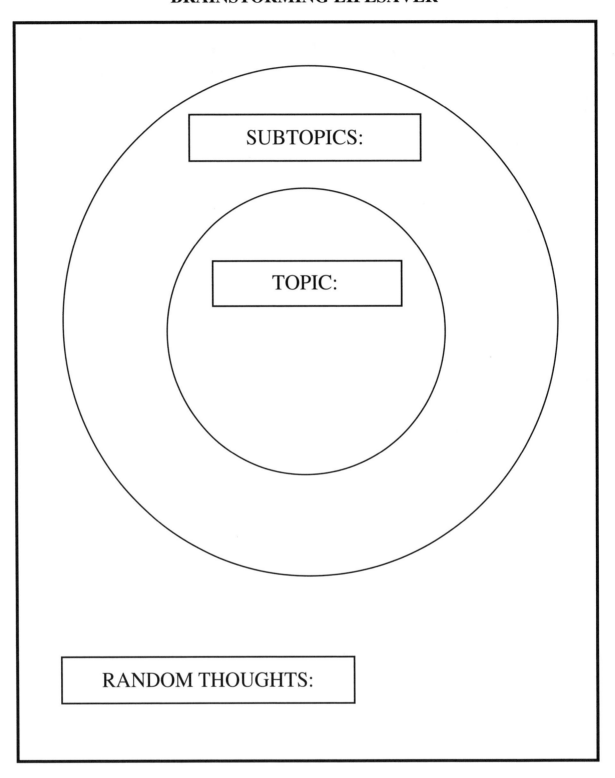

SUBTOPICS:

TOPIC:

RANDOM THOUGHTS:

Lifesaver Tool 54. Brainstorming Lifesaver

ON YOUR MARK, GET SET, GOAL!

Whether you're working to improve your professional or your personal life, setting goals is the best way to get there. Studies show that the majority of people don't set goals in life, but those who do are whoppingly more successful! Are you ready? Then let's "goal!"

Lifesaver Tips

L LIMIT
Limit yourself to five goals or fewer at a time.

I INTENTIONAL
Be intentional—review your goals daily.

F FULFILLING
Make sure your goals are worth fighting for.

E EXAMINE
Review your goals periodically to determine if changes need to be made.

S SPECIFIC
Be specific when setting goals. You can't make steps to reach those goals unless you're one-hundred-percent sure what they are.

A ATTAINABLE
Be realistic in your goals. Winning the lottery by the time you're forty would be great, but is it really attainable?

V VIGILANT
Strive vigilantly to meet your goals. Don't give up!

E END IN MIND
Set a reasonable deadline.

R RENEW
Don't work so hard on your goals that you neglect the most important part—you!

Lifesaver Trip 55:
Mind Tools Home Page

http://www.mindtools.com/

A toolbox full of gadgets to give your career—and life—a tune-up!

KEEPING TRACK OF YOUR GOALS

Professional	Personal
Goal:	Goal:
Steps:	Steps:
Resources Needed:	Resources Needed:
Progress Notes:	Progress Notes:
Deadline:	Deadline:

Lifesaver Tool 55. Keeping Track of Your Goals

"GOAL" FOR IT!

Just like exercise buddies, it's a lot more fun working toward a goal when you've got a little friendly support! This lifesaver helps you and your buddies meet your goals—don't "weight" to start it!

Lifesaver Tips

- At the beginning of the school year, put out a flyer announcing the formation of your goal group.

- If you prefer, just ask close friends or coworkers to join.

- Hold an informational meeting to explain the group's purpose.

- Hold meetings on the same day each month (e.g., the first school day of each month).

- Each member brings his or her own drink, a snack to share, and $5 to the meeting.

- Put the $5 each person brings into an envelope.

- During the meeting, each person shares any progress made during the previous month.

- Use the Goal Review Chart (Lifesaver Tool 56) to track progress on each goal.

- If desired, the group can spend time during the meeting discussing ways to overcome roadblocks.

- The person who has made the most progress gets the money envelope!

Lifesaver Trip 56: Motivation Home Page

http://www.motivation123.com/

Get hundreds of quick and easy motivational tips in this free monthly newsletter—you just have to be motivated to sign up!

GOAL REVIEW CHART

Goal Review	☺	☹	Progress Notes
Goal 1			
Goal 2			
Goal 3			
Goal 4			
Goal 5			

Lifesaver Tool 56. Goal Review Chart

BACK TO SCHOOL TIME

Do you want to get your master's degree or take a library science course, but don't really have the time (or desire) to go back to your old college campus? This lifesaver lets you know which classes are available online. Go to school in your jammies!

Lifesaver Tips: Eight Great Online Degree Programs:

- Drexel University (http://www.cis.Drexel.edu/)

- Kentucky Virtual University (http://www.kyvu.org/)

- The Indiana College Network (http://www.icn.org/index.html)

- Mansfield University (http://library.mnsfld.edu/schoolib.html)

- Southern Connecticut State University (http://www.southernct.edu/departments/ils)

- Syracuse University (http://istweb.syr.edu)

- University of Illinois at Urbana-Champaign (http://www.lis.uiuc.edu/gslis/degrees/leep.html)

- University of Pittsburgh (http://www.sis.pitt.edu/)

Library Trip 57:
World Wide Learn

http://www.worldwidelearn.com/library-science.htm

Get information on online degree programs and scholarship information and take a career assessment—"sea" if you need a new job.

TOP TEN LIST

Questions to Ask Before You Sign Up and Ship Out!

1.   Is the program accredited by the ALA?_____

2.   Is there a residency requirement?_____

3.   How many courses/hours does the program require?_____

4.   How much time do I have to complete the program?_____

5.   How much does the program cost? Each class?_____

6.   Is financial aid or a payment plan available?_____

7.   Are transfer credits accepted? If so, how many?_____

8.   Does the program offer job placement services?_____

9.   What is the deadline for registration? Registration fee? _____

10. Is the GRE required? Other paperwork?_____

Lifesaver Tool 57. Top Ten List

TRACK DOWN YOUR PROGRESS!

During the hectic school year, it's easy to forget all the workshops, in-service training, and other courses you've completed—by May, it's all a blur! Use this lifesaver to help you keep on track of your personal and professional development achievements before you race out the door for a great summer!

Lifesaver Tips

- Your superintendent will know you're super when you attach your track record (Lifesaver Tool 58) to your annual report. He or she will appreciate you going the extra mile.

- Don't forget to record personal and professional development—if it's not too personal, of course!

- The track record is divided into three sections: those attended, those conducted (you led the workshop), and those you facilitated (hosted).

- Give a copy to your principal at year's end to keep him or her on track!

Lifesaver Trip 58:
Leadership and the New Technologies Online Professional Development Workshops

http://www.edc.org/LNT/workshop.htm#General Information

Take free classes here to get your professional development on track—race to sign up!

PROFESSIONAL AND PERSONAL DEVELOPMENT TRACK RECORD

School Year:_____

Attended (Title and Date)	Conducted (Title and Date)	Facilitated (Title and Date)

Lifesaver Tool 58. Professional and Personal Development Track Record

R-E-F-L-E-C-T: FIND OUT WHAT IT MEANS TO ME!

Any time of year is a good time to reflect on your personal and professional development, but the beginning or end of the year is a perfect time to study your reflection and make sure your mirror is spot-free.

Lifesaver Tips

- For best results, use this lifesaver at the beginning, middle, and end of the year.

- Be honest when evaluating yourself.

- On the other hand, don't be too hard on yourself. (We're often our own worst critics.)

- After you complete the Self-Reflection (Lifesaver Tool 59), give it to a trusted colleague for a second opinion.

- Remember, the whole idea is to see how well you're working with others—nobody is perfect, and everyone has room for improvement.

- If you feel comfortable doing so, attach a copy of this Self-Reflection in your annual report.

Lifesaver Trip 59: Teacher Education Institute

http://www.teachereducation.com/course_outlines/graduate_online/ self_esteem_gradon_outline.htm

One of the many courses the Teacher Education Institute offers for graduate credit is "Self-Esteem for Educators," which encourages self-reflection. It may also improve what you see when you look in the mirror!

SELF-REFLECTION WORKSHEET

Directions: In each of the areas below, rate yourself by placing a 1 (*highest*) to 5 (*lowest*) in the appropriate box. Good luck!

I WORK WELL WITH STAFF	Date	Date	Date
I feel comfortable and confident dealing with other faculty.			
I enjoy coteaching and planning with other faculty.			
When there is a conflict with faculty, I deal with it quickly.			
Faculty members would say I am pleasant to work with.			
I WORK WELL WITH STUDENTS	Date	Date	Date
I am comfortable dealing with students of all abilities.			
I genuinely enjoy working with students.			
I feel comfortable disciplining students.			
I don't hold grudges with students.			
I WORK WELL WITH ADMINISTRATION	Date	Date	Date
I feel comfortable dealing with the principal and administrators.			
I can discuss concerns easily with my administration.			
I believe I have the support of my administration.			
The administration would say I am easy to work with.			
I WORK WELL WITH PARENTS	Date	Date	Date
I feel comfortable dealing with parents.			
I return parent calls promptly.			
I send newsletters, overdue notices, and other communications to parents.			
I have received few complaints from parents.			
HOW CAN I IMPROVE?			

Lifesaver Tool 59. Self-Reflection Worksheet

SHOULD YOU STAY OR SHOULD YOU GO NOW?

Whether you're going to the presentation or giving it, this lifesaver will come in handy when you need to evaluate a professional development program. It will help you "stay" a little more focused as the presenter "goes" on and on!

Lifesaver Tips

- This form can help others decide whether they should stay at or go to the program.

- In this time of tight funding, many schools want feedback following the workshop. Turn in the Stay or Go Form (Lifesaver Tool 60) after you leave.

- This form is also helpful to provide you with critical information following a workshop you have conducted or facilitated.

- Many grants require documentation; this evaluation tool can serve that purpose.

Lifesaver Trip 60:
How to Give a Talk

http://www.teachereducation.com/course_outlines/graduate_online/self_esteem_gradon_outline.htm

If you don't want your next audience to "go," read this informative article about giving effective presentations.

STAY OR GO FORM

NAME:_____

PRESENTATION:_____DATE:_____

I liked . . .

The best part . . .

The part I couldn't live without . . .

I loved . . .

I wish . . .

The part I didn't like was . . .

Lifesaver Tool 60. Stay or Go Form

SS 7

GO FISH! LIBRARY GAMES FOR ALL GRADE LEVELS

THE WEAKEST LIBRARY LINK

Who is the weakest link in your library? Find out when you play this fun learning game with students! (Sorry, Anne is not included!)

Lifesaver Tips

- Recommended Grade Level: 7–12

- Materials Needed:

  Large dry erase board to keep track of money earned and money banked
  Eight small dry erase boards for students to use to vote out the weakest link
  Questions (see Lifesaver Tool 61)

1. Choose eight students to participate (you may wish to draw names to be fair).

2. Each of the eight students sits in a circle at a large round table.

3. You, of course, are the host/inquisitor of the show.

4. Although the students are not strangers, the randomness of the draw will force the selected group to work as a team.

5. The rest of the class sits behind the table—close enough to see and hear.

6. Ask a capable student to write the following money figures on a dry erase board:

$$\textbf{\$1,000}$$
$$\textbf{\$2,000}$$
$$\textbf{\$3,000}$$
$$\textbf{\$4,000}$$
$$\textbf{\$5,000}$$

$6,000
$7,000
$8,000
$9,000
$10,000

Note: Bonus points could easily be substituted for dollar amounts (with teacher permission).

7.   The students work as a team to earn maximum prize money for each of six rounds of play.

8.   In the seventh round, the remaining contestants have a chance to double the bank.

9.   At the end of each round, contestants vote to eliminate the person who they feel is the weakest link.

10.   Each player is asked a "general knowledge" question.

11.   The host asks consecutive questions clearly and quickly, working clockwise around the circle of contestants.

12.   The goal in a round is for the team to answer enough questions correctly to earn as much money as possible.

13.   Each round ends when the players run out of time.

14.   Students may choose to bank money by clearly saying "bank" before the question is read. Money in the bank is safe.

15.   If students miss the question, the chain is broken and the team goes back to $0 and starts the chain over again.

16.   Lifesaver Tool 61 includes sources for book-related trivia questions.

17.   You can also write your own questions by putting the question on one side of the index question and the answer on the other.

18.   To write good trivia questions, see http://www.triviahalloffame.com/writeq.htm.

Lifesaver Trip 61:
The Weakest Link Home Page

http://www.nbc.com/Weakest_Link/rules.html

Go here for complete rules and show information—but watch out for Anne's brutal truths while you're there! After all, you don't want to be the weakest link!

FIVE LIFESAVERS FOR FINDING TRIVIA QUESTIONS

Literary Quizzes and Trivia: http://thinks.com/webguide/trivia/books.htm

Shakespeare Trivia: http://halife.com/teasers/shakespeare.html

Lord of the Rings Trivia Questions: http://www.bestkidsbooks.com

*Quiz Preparation Books: http://www.quizbowlonline.com/?source=googlequiz

Hemingway Trivia: http://www.timelesshemingway.com/hemtrivia.shtml

Note: You can always "link" to a great reference book, such as *The World Almanac* or *The World Almanac for Kids!*

Lifesaver Tool 61. Five Lifesavers for Finding Trivia Questions

YOUR FORMULA FOR FUN!

This lifesaver is a fun and easy way to encourage students to think. This formula = success!

Lifesaver Tips

- Recommended Grade Levels: 5–9

- Because this activity can be completed in five minutes or less, it's a great way to begin or end a library class.

- Use this activity at the beginning of the year to reinforce library policies.

- A variation on the activity is for students to write their own formulas.

- Giving a small prize (perhaps a book?) is always the formula for motivation!

Answer key: 1) 26 letters in the alphabet; 2) 10 parts of the Dewey Decimal Classification; 3) *10,000 Leagues Under the Sea*; 4) Two weeks in a checkout period; 5) 25 cents = overdue fine; 6) five-book limit; 7) *101 Dalmatians*; 8) Three Blind Mice; 9) Three Letters in a Call Number; 10) *Three Little Pigs*

Lifesaver Trip 62: Mind Teasers

http://www.geocities.com/brainteasergames/

These fun activities will blow your mind!

FORMULA WORKSHEET

Directions: See if you can figure out these fun formulas!

FORMULA	ANSWER
26 = L in A	
10 = Parts of DDC	
10,000 = L under the S	
*2 = W in a COP	
*$.25 = ODF	
*5 = BL	
101 = D	
3 = BM	
*3 = L in CN	
3 = LP	

* = formulas that may need to be changed to fit your library media center.

Lifesaver Tool 62. Formula Worksheet

GOT A GREAT LIBRARY GAME? GO FISH!

Your students will love going fishing in the library! Not your typical card game of fish, this game helps students catch Dewey numbers—line them up and reel in some great fun!

Lifesaver Tips

- Recommended Grade Levels: 5–9

- Divide class into teams of six players.

- Dealer (you or a designee) deals five cards to each player.

- Dealer places remaining cards face down in a pile.

- Choose a player to begin the game and take the first turn.

- A turn consists of a player asking for a specific type of card from another player's hand (e.g., "James, do you have any 900s?)

- To ask for a type of card (e.g., 900 card), the asking player must have at least one of those cards in his possession.

- The player must surrender all of those type of cards (e.g., 900s) to the player who asked for them.

- If the person asking was successful, that player gets another turn.

- If the person asked does not have that type of card (e.g., 900), he or she says "Go Fish!"

- The asker must then draw the top card off the pile.

- If the card drawn was the type that he or she asked for (e.g., 900), he shows the card to the other players and goes again.

- If the card drawn was not the type asked for, the player must keep the card.

- The person who said "Go Fish!" now gets a turn.

- The goal of the game is to collect as many "books" (four cards of the same type) as possible.

- As soon as a "book" is collected, it is placed face down in front of the player.

- The game continues until someone (or the pile) runs out of cards.

- The player who has the most books at the end of the game wins!

Lifesaver Trip 63:
Online Summer Games

http://www.kidsdomain.com/games/summer.html

Go fishing, coloring, or catching ocean surprises—"sea" how many great (free!) on-line games are here!

900s HISTORY AND GEOGRAPHY	**900s** HISTORY AND GEOGRAPHY
900s HISTORY AND GEOGRAPHY	**900s** HISTORY AND GEOGRAPHY
800s LITERATURE AND POETRY	**800s** LITERATURE AND POETRY
800s LITERATURE AND POETRY	**800s** LITERATURE AND POETRY
700s SPORTS, RECREATION AND LEISURE	**700s** SPORTS, RECREATION AND LEISURE
600s APPLIED SCIENCES COOKING AND HEALTH AND PETS	**600s** APPLIED SCIENCES COOKING AND HEALTH AND PETS

(Continued)

600s APPLIED SCIENCES COOKING AND HEALTH AND PETS	**600s** APPLIED SCIENCES COOKING AND HEALTH AND PETS
500s SCIENCE	**500s** SCIENCE
500s SCIENCE	**500s** SCIENCE
400s LANGUAGES	**400s** LANGUAGES
400s LANGUAGES	**400s** LANGUAGES
300s SOCIOLOGY	**300s** SOCIOLOGY
300s SOCIOLOGY	**300s** SOCIOLOGY

(Continued)

200s RELIGION	**200s** RELIGION
200s RELIGION	**200s** RELIGION
100s PHILOSOPHY	**100s** PHILOSOPHY
100s PHILOSOPHY	**100s** PHILOSOPHY
0-99s REFERENCE BOOKS	**0-99s** REFERENCE BOOKS
F/FIC FICTION	**F/FIC** FICTION
F/FIC FICTION	**F/FIC** FICTION

(Continued)

92/B BIOGRAPHY	**92/B** BIOGRAPHY
92/B BIOGRAPHY	**92/B** BIOGRAPHY
SC STORY COLLECTION	**SC** STORY COLLECTION
SC STORY COLLECTION	**SC** STORY COLLECTION
E EASY FICTION	**E** EASY FICTION
E EASY FICTION	**E** EASY FICTION

Lifesaver Tool 63. Go Fish!

Library Lifesaver 64

WHO WANTS TO BE A MILLIONAIRE?

The students might not get a million dollars of cold, hard cash for winning this game, but they might get a million laughs! This adaptation of the popular TV show is a great way to be rich in knowledge!

Lifesaver Tips

- Recommended Grade Levels: 7–12.

- Begin the game by having a class lightning round. Ask the entire class the same question (by the way, you are Regis!). The person who answers the question correctly in the shortest amount of time goes on to the next stage of the competition.

- The first student in the "hot seat" answers multiple-choice questions until that student guesses incorrectly. The student is then eliminated from the competition.

- On the other hand, the student may choose to stop playing to keep all points won.

- If the student quits, another lightning round is played to get another eligible contestant.

- The student has three lifelines available:

    Lifeline 1: Ask the audience—the student asks members of the audience to write down their guesses. The player then decides if he or she wants to go with the majority or pick his or her own answer.

    Lifeline 2: Phone a Friend—the student can call a friend to help answer the question in a thirty-second time limit (phoning the principal is a hoot!).

    Lifeline 3: Fifty-Fifty Chance—Two answers are eliminated, and the player chooses one of the two remaining answers.

The idea is to use the lifelines for the tough questions to get as many points as possible.

- You can make up your own prizes to give students something to work for—a million dollars probably won't be an option!

- It's really fun to have class competitions to see which class can earn the most points by the end of the year.

- Copy plenty of "Who Wants to Be a Millionaire" handouts (Lifesaver Tool 64) to keep track of the score earned. Use a different handout for each player.

- To get great questions, ask teachers for multiple-choice workbook questions the students have covered in classes.

- Another great source of questions is to have the older students make up questions for the younger players—it's a great learning activity!

Lifesaver Trip 64:
Who Wants to Play Millionaire Online?

http://www.millionairequizsite.co.uk/OIO1.htm

It's not the official site, but unofficially, it's a lot of fun! Have your students put in their two cents here as a warm-up before the game begins!

"WHO WANTS TO BE A MILLIONAIRE" HANDOUTS

$1 MILLION DOLLARS!!!
$500,000
$250,000
$125,000
$64,000
$32,000
$16,000
$8,000
$4,000
$2,000
$1,000
$500
$300
$200
$100
START HERE

* ***Bold face dollar amounts*** represent money that can be kept if the contestant stops.

Lifesaver Tool 64. "Who Wants to Be a Millionaire" Handouts

Library Lifesaver 65

LIBRARY WIN, LOSE—AND DRAW!

There are no real losers when you play this fun library game!

Lifesaver Tips

- Recommended Grade Levels: 5–9

- Divide the class into two teams (I designate a purple team and a white team in honor of our school colors).

- Choose someone from the purple team to draw.

- The student selected chooses a card (from Lifesaver Tool 65).

- The purple team has one minute to guess the library-related clue as the student draws.

- If the purple teammates guess correctly, they earn five points.

- If they guess incorrectly or time runs out, the white team gets a chance to guess.

- The game continues with alternating teams drawing until time runs out.

- The team that has the most points at the end of the class wins a prize (I often use bonus points and let teams select a book from Scholastic). On the other hand—chocolate (or a soft drink) is always a favorite prize.

- Deduct points from teams if they get too loud.

Lifesaver Trip 65: Cartoon Critters

http://www.cartooncritters.com/

Students can draw, read a story, find jokes and riddles—whether they win or lose, this is a great online site!

LIBRARY WIN, LOSE—AND DRAW! CARDS

Library win, lose—and draw! **Clue: Rumplestiltskin**	Library win, lose—and draw! **Clue: Peter Pan**
Library win, lose—and draw! **Clue: Mother Goose**	Library win, lose—and draw! **Clue: Princess Bride**
Library win, lose—and draw! **Clue: biography**	Library win, lose—and draw! **Clue: Hansel and Gretel**
Library win, lose—and draw! **Clue: index**	Library win, lose—and draw! **Clue: atlas**
Library win, lose—and draw! **Clue: Internet home page**	Library win, lose—and draw! **Clue: bibliography**
Library win, lose—and draw! **Clue: author**	Library win, lose—and draw! **Clue: illustrator**
Library win, lose—and draw! **Clue: table of contents**	Library win, lose—and draw! **Clue: clip art**
Library win, lose—and draw! **Clue: series**	Library win, lose—and draw! **Clue: bookend**
Library win, lose—and draw! **Clue: circulation desk**	Library win, lose—and draw! **Clue: periodical**

Lifesaver Tool 65. Library Win, Lose—and Draw! Cards

LIBRARY TIC-TAC-TOE

Lifesaver Tips

- Recommended Grade Levels: 5–9.

- Place the tic-tac-toe transparency (Lifesaver Tool 66) on the overhead projector.

- Divide class into two groups: Xs and Os.

- Ask reference-type questions to students.

- Members of the X team go first. If they answer the question correctly, they get to choose where they want the "X" placed.

- Obviously, teammates will need to work together to get answers and block out the other team.

- The first team to have three Xs or Os in a row (horizontally, vertically, or diagonally) earns twenty-five points.

- Play as many tic-tac-toe games as possible in a class period.

Lifesaver Trip 66:
Tic-Tac-Toe Online

http://boulter.com/ttt/index.cgi

Play tic-tac-toe—go, go, go!

LIBRARY TIC-TAC-TOE!

Lifesaver Tool 66. Library Tic-Tac-Toe!

THE PRICE IS RIGHT!

If you're a librarian, you know firsthand how expensive books can be. This lifesaver is not only a fun game to play, it's a great tool to help students understand and appreciate the cost of books.

Lifesaver Tips

- Recommended Grade Levels: 7–12

- Draw the names of four contestants from the audience (class) to begin the game.

- The first four students step up to the podiums (a great way to help students to get comfortable in front of an audience).

- Ask an assistant (student or teacher) to bring out the first book. (Choose books in a variety of formats and from a variety of copyright dates to show students how the cost of books have increased over the years.)

- Students write their bids on a dry erase board.

- You act as host and call on each student to show you their guesses as to what the book originally cost.

- The student closest to the actual price (without going over) proceeds to the next round of competition.

- The student who guesses correctly sits in the winner's circle and waits for three other teammates.

- Choose another name to fill the empty spot.

- Ask the assistant to bring out the next book.

- The game continues in this way until four contestants have been chosen.

- The four contestants are given book trivia questions to answer. Because this game focuses on prices of books, I ask questions relating to those books. For example, title, author, and character names are great questions to ask.

- If the contestant cannot answer a question, he or she may choose one audience member to assist.

- A contestant earns a point for every question guessed correctly in a thirty-second time limit.

Lifesaver Trip 67:
The Price Is Right!

http://www.cbs.com/daytime/price/

Visit the virtual Bob Barker here and read his bio! (Oh, by the way, don't forget to get your pet spayed or neutered!)

THE PRICE IS (NOT!) RIGHT FOR BOOKS!

Sample Prices

Reference-single volume
    The New Oxford American Dictionary (2001)
        Retail: $50.00

Reference set
    Encyclopaedia Britannica Print Set and Yearbook (2002)
        Retail: $1,295.00

Fiction—paperback
    A Painted House by John Grisham (2001)
        Retail: $7.99

Fiction—hardback
    Cirque Du Freak: The Vampire's Assistant by Daren Shan (2001)
        Retail: $15.99

Nonfiction—hardback
    The Underground Guide to Teenage Sexuality by Michael J. Basso (1997)
        Retail: $14.95

Nonfiction—hardback
    Life Strategies for Teens by Jay McGraw
        Retail: $19.99

Out of print book
    Gift from the Sea by Anne Morrow Lindbergh (20th anniversary edition, 1975)
        Retail: $3.95

Nonfiction—technical
    Ocp: Oracle9i Certification Kit by Chip Dawes (2002)
        Retail: $149.96

Lifesaver Tool 67. The Price Is (Not!) Right for Books!

BOGGLE THEIR MINDS!

It boggles my mind why I never thought of using this game in the media center before! I've always enjoyed playing this classic word game with my family but never thought about using it at school until recently. I don't "mind" saying—this game spells fun!

Lifesaver Tips

- Recommended Grade Levels: 7–12

- You can play this game with a group in two ways. One way is to purchase five games and play in small groups. The other is to use one game and use a flex cam to project the game on the large screen for all to see. Either way, the rules are the same.

- Shake up the boggle game pieces.

- Turn over the timer and say "Go!"

- Students have three minutes to form as many words of three letters or more as they can.

- Letters must be touching (diagonal, up, down, sideways).

- Students may not use a letter twice.

- I bend the rules a little and allow proper nouns (e.g., names, places).

- Students earn points for words they find that no one else does (e.g., If Johnny and Joe both find the word "house," they both cross the word "house" off their list, and neither gets a point for that word).

- Students earn one point for three-letter and four -letter word.

- Students earn two points for five-letter words.

- Students earn five points for words of six or more letters.

- Students must remain quiet when the timer ends the game. One at a time they each read the words off their lists.

- I deduct points if students are not listening because it delays the game to have to repeat words.

- For an added incentive, I count library-related words double. The only catch is I am the judge and only I can decide if it's a library-related word (this prevents arguing!).

- The student with the most points at the end of the game (i.e., class period) wins.

- Any student who spells DEWEY automatically wins, and the game is over.

Lifesaver Trip 68:
Boggle!

http://www.centralconnector.com/GAMES/boggle.html

Go here to find complete rules and game information—or just use the rules I've made up if the rules "boggle" your mind!

LIBRARY BOGGLE!

U	H	*E*	*S*
L	*T*	*R*	*U*
K	*O*	R	W
A	*O*	N	A

Sample Game—Words Found:

TOO

WARN

SURE

- If this had been a real game, I would have scored three points (one point for each word) if no other players found the same words.

- If I chose to challenge the judge, I could try to earn double points for the word "warn" because the librarian always warns students to be quiet. (It's up to you, as judge, to accept the challenge or not!)

Lifesaver Tool 68. Library Boggle!

THIS GAME HAS A MONOPOLY ON FUN!

Who doesn't love to play a great game of Monopoly? Whenever you're students are "board," pull out this game. They'll be having fun and learning library skills before you can say "Park Avenue!"

Lifesaver Tips

- Recommended Grade Levels: 7–12
- Because of the extensive time involved in this game, you may need to play over two or three consecutive class periods.
- This game is played according to traditional Monopoly rules—with a few changes.
- Any student who lands on Reading Railroad automatically gets all money in the bank—no matter who owns the property.
- If a student has all four pieces of property, he or she is eligible to earn a house or hotel.
- To earn a house, the student must find information about that property in an atlas, an encyclopedia, or on an Internet site (see Lifesaver Tool 69).
- To earn a hotel, the student must find information in all three sources (atlas, encyclopedia, and Internet).
- The student who accumulates the most money, property, houses, and hotels at the end of the specified time wins.

Lifesaver Trip 69: eBay!

http://www.eBay.com

Browse through eBay's bookstore if you want to find an out of print or hard to find book. You'll want to bookmark this amazing site of 30,000+ books. eBay certainly has the "monopoly" on online buying and selling!

MEDIA MONOPOLY GAME

Name:_____Class:_____

Property:_____

Source(s):

Encyclopedia page_____

Atlas page_____

Internet http:_____

Fact:

I wish to purchase a house hotel

Lifesaver Tool 69. Media Monopoly Game

FISH FOR A GREAT BOOK

You'll always catch a great book in the media center! Unfortunately, sometimes students need a little bait to get them to read. This is a game they'll fall for—hook, line, and sinker!

Lifesaver Tips

- Recommended Grade Levels: 5–9

- Divide students into five groups. You can allow students to choose their own groups or assign them to groups—whichever works best for you.

- Give each group an envelope containing five questions. (Each question contains clues about books.)

- Students must work cooperatively to solve the puzzle and locate the mystery books.

- When (and if!) students discover the correct book, they will find a "fish" in the pocket.

- The first group to catch all five fish is declared the winner.

- Throw fish back if the group is too noisy or does not work well together as a team.

- The "school" of thought here is teamwork and cooperation.

- I have tried to use questions "generic" enough to suit all libraries (Lifesaver Tool 70). Before beginning the activity, ask a student helper to go fish for the books and write down the call numbers for you.

- It's fun for older students to make up clues for younger students if you want more of a "mess" of fish!

Lifesaver Trip 70:
Fish Warp!

http://members.aol.com/bassratter/fishwarp.htm

A creative online game that lets players click and drag to change the size of the fish—a great way to get young fisherman used to the mouse!

GO FISH! QUESTIONS

Group 1 Questions

Q. A book about a blind girl with the first name of Helen.

A. _____

Q. A fairy tale about a sleepy princess.

A. _____

Q. A biography about George Washington.

A. _____

Q. A story about a beautiful black horse.

A. _____

Q. A *World Book Atlas.*

A. _____

Group 2 Questions

Q. A book about Abraham Lincoln.

A. _____

Q. A story about a faithful yellow dog.

A. _____

Q. A *Webster's Dictionary.*
A. _____

Q. A basketball book by Dygard.
A. _____

Q. A drawing book by Emberly.
A. _____

Group 3 Questions

Q. The *World Almanac* (most recent edition).
A. _____

(Continued)

Q. A fairy tale about a big bad wolf.

A. _____

Q. A book by Shel Silverstein with "light" in the title.

A. _____

Q. A Mother Goose book.

A. _____

Q. The first book R. L. Stine wrote.

A. _____

Group 4 Questions

Q. A biography on President Kennedy.

A. _____

Q. A book about all the presidents.

A. _____

Q. A *Webster's Dictionary*.

A. _____

Q. A book by Gary Paulsen about a type of weapon.

A. _____

Q. A book by C. S. Lewis about a lion.

A. _____

Group 5 Questions

Q. A rhyming dictionary.

A. _____

Q. Today's newspaper.

A. _____

Q. A book about President Eisenhower.

A. _____

Q. A book on race cars.

A. _____

Q. A book on sign language.

A. _____

(Continued)

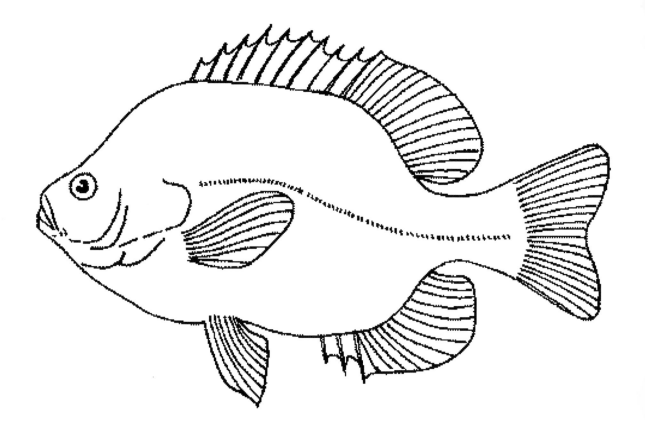

Lifesaver Tool 70. Go Fish!

Image © 2002-2003 www.clipart.com

SS 8

"SEA" WHAT OTHERS ARE DOING—LIBRARY MEDIA CENTER BEST PRACTICES

SHE'S TURNING JAPANESE!

Bonnie Heile, Library Media Specialist

Professional Experience

- Eleven years at North Attleborough High School in Massachusetts (Nineteen years in education)

Honors

- Fulbright Memorial Teacher Fund Scholar 2002 (awarded three-week sabbatical in Japan)

- TCI Teacher Scholar (received professional leave for conference held in Denver, Colorado)

- Global Educator Award 2002 for Outstanding Performance on "A Look at China and Japan" Project

- Southeast Area Director for Massachusetts School Library Media Association

Lifesaver Tips: Best Practices

- Close Collaboration with Teachers

    "Teachers know they can come to the media center and the staff will come up with or define an idea. I often each lunch with teachers I'm working with and visit their classroom to get more of a feel for a project.

- Take Advantage of Skills and Abilities of Staff Members

  "My personal interest in Japan and China has been the start of several projects. My partner's special interest is in young adult literature. She is now the "Book Talk Lady!" Our paraprofessional is a whiz on Excel. We now have great statistics for the media center. By taking advantage of each person's special abilities, the results have become better and better!"

- Remember, You Are a Teacher, Too

  "Take advantage of courses wherever you may find them—whether they are offered by the district, at a local college, or even across the hall! Some of the courses I have benefited from are Skillful Teacher, local district computer courses, and Asian [history] courses at a local university. Take advantage of opportunities to become a lifelong learner!"

- Advice to Newbies

  "You can't do it all the first week or month or even year! Pick several areas you want to work and concentrate solely on those areas. Don't worry—you'll never run out of projects! When you first enter the profession, find another librarian to be your mentor. This is especially important if you work alone. Ours is a unique profession. You need a colleague to validate concerns, answer questions, or just lend a shoulder in times of need. In our district, school librarians and public librarians meet together on a regular basis. It works."

- It's a Laugh

  "One of the history teachers sent a student to the media center to get information. When the student returned, she asked who helped find the needed answers. The student replied, 'The Japanese One!' I had just returned from my Fulbright experience. Since I am blonde, I didn't realize that I had absorbed enough of the culture to become Japanese. Learning is really skin deep!"

Lifesaver Trip 71

bheile@yahoo.com

http://www.naschools.net/nahsmc

"So many books . . . so little time!"

Bonnie Heile's
FAVORITE FIVE

Favorite Professional Book?
Any title written by another librarian who knows!

Favorite Read-Aloud?
How Droofus the Dragon Lost His Head **by Bill Peet**

Favorite Web Site? (Follett Titlewave)
http://www.flr.follett.com/login/

Favorite Search Engine?
Google

Favorite Company?
Amazon.com and Half.com

Lifesaver Tool 71. Favorite Five, Bonnie Heile

AT YOUR SERVICE!

Diane Mentzer, Library Media Specialist, Technology Coordinator, Webmaster

Professional Experience

- Nineteen years at Paramount Elementary School Library Media Center, Waynesboro, Pennsylvania

Honors

- 2000 County Computer Educator of the Year

- Maryland Technology Academy Fellow (top one hundred chosen out of seven hundred applicants)

- Completing Requirements for National Board Certification, Library Media Specialist

Lifesaver Tips: Best Practices

- Get Involved with Web Design:

    "I serve as the school's webmaster. I know our Web site is one of the best in the county. I have pages for each teacher and post links, hotlists, and other important information for them. This makes it easier for the students to be able to access the information they need—both at school and at home. I also put a lot of pictures on the site, which allows parents to participate in school activities even when they are working."

- Train Your Students

"I have my students return their books and reshelve them. This helps reinforce book location and Dewey Decimal skills we have learned. It also saves valuable time. Although the students aren't always perfect, they do a great job and are so proud of what they are able to do. Recently, I heard from a parent that her daughter, who had changed to another school, gave her new school an "8" for the first day. Her mother asked her why the new school ranked so high, and the student excitedly shared that when the new librarian was teaching book location, she already knew because she had been 'doing it for years!' This pride in doing raises self-esteem and teaches responsibility and independence."

- Help Your Teachers

"I consider the assistance I give teachers to be one of my best practices. I help put the elementary curriculums in the Internet. As a result, I am very knowledgeable about each grade's curriculum and standards. Having this inside knowledge allows me to serve each teacher personally by forwarding listserv messages, clipping and sending content-related magazine articles, and posting relevant links on the teacher's Internet site. Teachers who leave my school often return to tell me how much they miss this personal service!"

- Advice to Newbies

"My advice is simple—make friends with the school secretary, custodian, and other special teachers ASAP!"

- It's a Laugh

"I once had a little boy say that he hoped the teacher didn't come back and pick them up because then he could go home and sleep with me! He wanted to do this because he was sure I knew a lot of bedtime stories!" Thankfully, the teacher did return!

Lifesaver Trip 72

mentzdia@wcboe.k12.md.us

http://www.wcboe.k12.mad.us/manifold/schoopag/elementary/paramount/index.html

"Show me a computer expert that gives a damn, and I'll show you a librarian!" (Patricia Wilson Berger)

Diane Mentzer's
FAVORITE FIVE

Favorite Professional Book?
Elementary School Librarian's Survival Guide

Favorite Read-Aloud?
The Library Dragon by Carmen Agra Deedy

Favorite Web Site?
Kathy Schrock's Guide to Educators site:
http://school.discovery.com/shrockguide/

Favorite Search Engine?
Google

Favorite Company?
Gumdrop, Library Video Company, Boise Cascade

Lifesaver Tool 72. Favorite Five, Diane Mentzer

Library Lifesaver 73

COVER STORY!

Pamela Nutt, Library Media Specialist

Professional Experience

- Six years at Moore Elementary School Media Center in Locust Grove, Georgia (Ten years in education)

Honors

- May 2002 *School Library Journal* (cover feature!)

- 2002 Teacher of the Year at Moore Elementary School

- 2002 Spaulding County Teacher of the Year

- 2002 Graduate Student in Instructional Technology (University of West Georgia)

- Henry County School Board Member

- Governor's Appointee to Professional Standards Board Commission

- 2002 Georgia Media Specialist of the Year (Wow!)

Lifesaver Tips: Best Practices

- Empower Others

    "Empower as many people as you can to do tasks that you cannot always do yourself. Train older students to check out books, shelve, and run equipment. Fully utilize your student resources!"

- Visit Classrooms Daily

    "Take the time to visit at least one classroom a day. Spend a few precious minutes seeing what students are learning and teachers are teaching. This practice only takes a few minutes, and it's invaluable for ordering and curriculum design."

- Eat Lunch in the Cafeteria

    "This advice may sound simplistic, but it helps to form a bond with teachers and students. I, for too long, ate in the media center to keep it open. My associate and I now take turns eating to give us time to get out and mingle!"

- Send Out Surveys. "Ask teachers what they would like to see continued, added, or changed—especially if you're new to the job. This input is invaluable!"

- Never Stop Learning

    "I am currently working on my doctorate. I believe that the more I learn, the more I have to share with my fellow teachers and students. Don't be afraid to try something new!"

- Advice to Newbies

    "Don't be afraid to say 'No!' We, as educators, tend to work hard and allow people to give us more than we can possibly do. The next time someone asks you to take on a new project or serve on a committee, say no! If just saying no is too hard, tell them maybe next time. This does not close doors completely, but leaves them cracked."

- It's a Laugh

    "I work in an inner-city school. One of my kids came to the library and listened as I read, *I Took My Frog to the Library*. I changed the characters in the book with me bringing the animals and my associate being the librarian. With much disappointment, a child said, 'Ms. Nutt, Ms. Freeman should have spanked you for bringing all those animals in the place! You better be glad you don't live at my house!'"

Lifesaver Trip 73

pnutt@mindspring.com

http://www.henry.k12.ga.us

"If everyone is thinking alike, then someone is not thinking!"

Pamela Nutt's
FAVORITE FIVE

Favorite Professional Book?
Information Power

Favorite Read-Aloud?
The Very Hungry Caterpillar and
Click, Clack, Moo, Cows That Type

Favorite Web Site?
http://www.teach-ology.com
http://www.ala.org

Favorite Search Engine?
Google and Dogpile

Favorite Company?
Bound To Stay Bound

Lifesaver Tool 73. Favorite Five, Pamela Nutt

SKIRTING LIBRARY ISSUES

Heidi Graham, Library Media Specialist

Professional Experience

- Sixteen years as a media specialist at New Smyrna Beach High School in Florida (Thirty-three years in education)

Honors

- Teacher of the Quarter

- Golden Apple Award Recipient

- New Smyrna Beach High School 2003 Teacher of the Year

Lifesaver Tips: Best Practices

- High School Booktalks

  "I've found that often students want to read, but usually choose the wrong book. Booktalking gives me an 'in,' so they come to me for book suggestions. I am pretty good at 'hooking' the student with the 'right' book. This also ensures that I read a tremendous amount of books, especially fiction. Both the teachers and the students like the book suggestions I give!"

- Play Stations

    "Actually students don't play at these stations, but they don't know it yet! I work with teachers to develop six to eight centers for activities to introduce, explain, or provide an overview of a topic they are, or will be, studying. At each station, teams of students produce a product or write a response. The stations encompass about three days in the media center. The students really enjoy the stations and often don't realize they're learning as they 'play' at the stations."

- Web Evaluations

    "I developed a Web evaluation when students use Internet sources. The in-depth evaluation shows samples of good and bad Web pages and explains a reverse search strategy. These Web evaluations help the students learn to swim—not sink when doing Internet research!"

- Advice to Newbies

    "Laugh, love, and work!"

- It's a Laugh

    "My funniest moment occurred during my first year of teaching (although it certainly wasn't funny at the time!). My then assistant principal said that a parent had complained that my skirts were too short. To check, he made me kneel on the floor to measure the distance from my hem to the floor. I was in compliance, but also in tears!"

Lifesaver Trip 74

hegraham@mail.volusia.k12.fl.us

http://www.newsmymahigh.org

"Just Do It!" (Nike)

Heidi Graham's
FAVORITE FIVE

Favorite Professional Book?
I Read It, But I Don't Get It **by Chris Tovani?**

Favorite Read-Aloud?
Shel Silverstein's Books!

Favorite Web Site?
http://www.bcps.org/offices/lis/office/partner.html/

Favorite Search Engine?
Google

Favorite Company?
Publisher's Quality Library Service

Lifesaver Tool 74. Favorite Five, Heidi Graham

INFOQUEST—THE BEST!

Peggy S. Milam, Library Media Specialist

Professional Experience

Eight years as library media specialist at Compton Elementary School in Powder Springs, Georgia (twenty-five years in education)

Honors:

- 1999 Student Services Award

- 2000 Extra Mile Award

- 2001 Media Leadership Team Member

- 2002 Taiwan International Conference on Information Literacy Speaker (Canceled due to the terrorist attacks on September 11, 2001)

Lifesaver Tips: Best Practices

- InfoQuest

    "My best practice is a research game I invented to teach information literacy skills from kindergarten through twelfth grade and even college. (InfoQuest is detailed in my book, *InfoQuest: A New Twist on Information Literacy* by Linworth Publishing, 2002). Each week we ask a challenging library research questions with the morning announcements. Students have all week to locate the answer in the media center. The questions are designed to correlate with the curriculum and focus on developing higher-order thinking and problem-solving skills. Students who participate regularly meet all the information literacy standards in our district and become familiar with all varieties of research materials, both print and nonprint. This program has been presented at the Conference on

Children's Literature at the University of Georgia and at the Independent School in Atlanta, Georgia. This educational activity is now used in a number of school districts across the state and is even spreading around the country!"

- Compton Cubs are W.I.L.D.

   "This W.I.L.D. (Winning at Information Literacy Development) activity focuses on reading, writing, and research at our school and prepares students for the jump to middle school. Students are wild about it, too!"

- Book Swap

   "I began a book swap at our school for families to trade in lightly read books two for one. As a result, we now have a continuous cycle of new titles for students and parents to read!"

- Advice to Newbies

   "Go in like a lamb! Native Americans taught that there is great power in humility!"

- It's a Laugh

   "My funny story is a 'last laugh!' A former administrator told me that we could never draw kids into the media center by asking a challenging research question. In her words, 'That will never work!' Yet the first year it became so popular that the PTO got involved and donated more than $16,000 for new books. Now, we're laughing all the way to the bank!"

Lifesaver Trip 75

peggymilam@hotmail.com

www.cobb.k12.ga.us/~compton

   "Do unto others as you would have them do unto you!" (The Golden Rule)

Peggy S. Milam's
FAVORITE FIVE

Favorite Professional Book?
Do I Have To Pick Just One?

Favorite Read-Aloud?
Frindle **by Andrew Clement**

Favorite Web Site?
http://www.bcps.org/offices/lis/office/partner.html/

Favorite Search Engine?
Google

Favorite Company?
Publisher's Quality Library Service

Lifesaver Tool 75. Favorite Five, Peggy S. Milam

SAMPLE THE BEST!

Debra L. Samples, Media Specialist

Professional Experience

- Four years as media specialist at Ben Davis Junior High School in Indianapolis, Indiana

- Four years as media specialist at F. J. Reitz High School in Evansville, Indiana

- Twenty-one total years of experience in education

Honors

- 2002 Ben Davis Junior High School Teacher of the Year

- 2002 Wayne Township Extra Mile Award Winner

Lifesaver Tips: Best Practices

- Smile!

    "Each day I remind myself that, even for a brief moment, I may be the only positive force in that student's life. My smile and kind words may be the only ones the student hears today. Remembering this gives me a sense of mission every day!" In addition, although grandchildren are on a very distant horizon, I remind myself that students in the media center are a bit like grandchildren. I do not have to raise them, just love them and send them back to their teachers!"

- Respect!

  "Respect your students by listening to them. Trust in what their interests are. Buy what they like whenever possible!"

- Piggyback!

  "At every opportunity, piggyback! Like most schools, I have no budget for guest authors, but through connections with bookstores and our outstanding public library, our students have met renown authors such as Katherine Paterson, Richard Peck, Sheila Carson Levine, Christopher Paul Curtis, and many more—at little or no cost! I believe author encounters can change lives."

- Advice to Newbies

  "Most media specialists serve as the "one and only" in their schools. Find a mentor who can help keep you motivated, focused, and provide a shoulder to lean on. Few faculty members will ever understand the challenges of the "easy" job we have!"

- It's a Laugh

  "I have had many "funniest moments." It's easier for me to name my funnest moment, which is, undoubtedly, meeting authors—especially Mary Higgins Clark. I can only hope to live as long as she and be as eloquent and gracious.

- Last Words

  "It is all too tempting to forget that most of our duties are described as library or media *services*. Never forget our mission is to *serve* our students, parents, faculty, and staff!"

Lifesaver Trip 76

debra.samples@wayne.k12.in.us

http://www.wayne.k12.in.us

"Once you learn to read, you will be forever free" (Frederick Douglass)

Debra L. Samples's
FAVORITE FIVE

Favorite Professional Book?
Teaching with Love & Logic by Jim Fay
Parenting with Love & Logic by Jim Fay

Favorite Read-Aloud?
Something Beautiful by Sharon Dennis Wyeth

Favorite Web Site?
http://www.amazon.com

Favorite Search Engine?
Google

Favorite Company?
Demco, Follett & Perma-Bound

Lifesaver Tool 76. Favorite Five, Debra L. Samples

"NEED" A GREAT MEDIA SPECIALIST? HERE SHE IS!

Miriam Walrath Needham, Library Media Specialist

Professional Experience

- Twenty-six years in library media (Twenty-nine years in education)

Honors

- Jim Harbin Student Media Festival Awards (local, state, and regional levels)

- ACET Excellence in Media Production Awards

- 1998 Teacher of the Year at Dr. N. H. Jones Elementary School in Ocala, Florida

Lifesaver Tips: Best Practices

- Young Author's Day

    "At this author celebration, every student in the building writes and illustrates a story, which is bound into a book. We then hold a huge celebration for all of our aspiring authors. Several famous authors have attended Young Author's Day, such as Elvira Woodruff, Jack Gantos, Tedd Arnold, Peter Catalanotto, and Megan McDonald. On this special day we have sessions running concurrently for students to rotate through. Sessions include author sessions, story sessions, and, my favorite, the author's chair session in which students get to share what they have written with their peers. This celebration is a culmination of writing efforts throughout the year, and students look forward to it every year!"

- Panther Prime Time

  "This is our award-winning morning show. The news show is completely student written, and produced and directed by students. We have student anchors deliver the show three days per week. Our school has won numerous local, state, and national awards for this program. Our show is even featured on a local cable educational access channel. One of the reasons for this show's success is because our school is a math, science, technology (and now media production!) magnet school.

- Sunshine Book Bowl

  "This is a countywide academic bowl. Participating teams from eighteen to twenty elementary schools answer question about the fifteen Sunshine State books. This year marks our seventh Book Bowl!"

- Advice to Newbies

  "Find a mentor—the advice of an experienced library media specialist is invaluable!"

- It's a Laugh

  "My funniest moment occurred in 1987 during Children's Book Week. Our theme for that year was "Pig Out on Books!" I arranged for a farmer friend to bring a pig to the library for the day for the children to visit. The pig arrived early that morning in a large truck and, much to my surprise, the pig was not a cute little piggy—but rather a great, big, ugly hog! As my farmer friend waved goodbye, he left strict instructions to get the hog out of the truck as soon as possible because of the heat. My small box that I'd neatly arranged in the library was not going to work. With the help of the P.E. teacher, we took the hog to the fenced in kindergarten playground. With a water hose, we made him a comfortable mud hole and invited the children to visit him there. Throughout the day, he had many visitors and was even able to enjoy delicious cafeteria food. Close to dismissal time, my assistant went to check in on him—only to find the mud hole deserted and the playground empty. The hog had escaped his temporary "hog heaven!" We called in all the troops (our janitor and teachers) to help us round up and "hog tie" our escapee. We finally managed to capture "piggly wiggly" after quite a chase! The students, of course, went "hog wild!"

Lifesaver Trip 77

needhamm@marion.k12.fl.us

http://www.firn.edu/schools/marion/nhjones

"What a school feels about its library is a measure of what it feels about education!"

Miriam Walrath Needham's
FAVORITE FIVE

Favorite Professional Book?
Information Power

Favorite Read-Aloud?
The Little House **(Virginia Lee Burton)**
Old Black Fly **(Jim Aylesworth)**
Officer Buckle and Gloria **(Peggy Rathman)**

Favorite Web Site?
http://www.sunlink.ucf.edu/
(Florida's K–12 database)

Favorite Search Engine?
Google

Favorite Company?
Bound to Stay Bound

Lifesaver Tool 77. Favorite Five, Miriam Walrath Needham

IF YOU CAN'T BEAT 'EM, JOIN 'EM!

Carl A. Harvey II, Library Media Specialist

Professional Experience

- Five years experience as library media specialist

- One year at North Elementary School, Noblesville, Indiana

- Four years at Lowell Elementary School in Metropolitan School District of Warren Township, Indianapolis, Indiana

Honors

- 2001 IPALCO Golden Apple Award

- 2000 AASL Frances Henne Award

- 1999 Outstanding New Library Media Specialist (Indiana Library Federation)

- Presenter at numerous local, state, and national conferences

Lifesaver Tips: Best Practices

- Research Stations

    "To help focus students during research and to expose them to a variety of resources, my students use stations to rotate between resources. This makes sure everyone gets his or her turn at the computer, but also a chance to look for print information."

- Collaboration Projects

    "In honor and support of 'Read Across America Day,' our school participates in a multischool, multidistrict reading program entitled 'Read across the City!'

- Staff Development

  "I enjoy working on professional development opportunities to support teachers in collaboration and technology integration. Some of my presentations and projects can be found on my library media center Web page."

- Advice to Newbies

  "Get involved in your state library media association. Network with colleagues in your district and in the state. They will be invaluable resources to you! Currently, I'm involved in eight professional organizations and committees."

- It's a Laugh

  "I was in a car crash at the corner of the school where I student taught. I stopped traffic for a few hours. While my car was totaled, I opted to stay at school since I was ok. I was working with a class in the library media center and one of the teachers explained to her class about the car crash. A second grader raised his hand and said, "At least you weren't killed!" Young ones can certainly put things into perspective for us!"

- Last Words

  "I've published several professional articles, including 'It Takes Two: Media & You," *School Library Media Activities Monthly* (March 2002); 'It's Research, Dear Watson,' *School Library Media Activities Monthly* (December 2001); 'Read across the City,' *School Library Media Activities Monthly* (March 2001); 'Baby Bytes: Integrating Technology Effectively,' *School Library Media Activities Monthly* (November 1999). My advice, obviously, is to share your knowledge!"

Lifesaver Trip 78

carl_harvey@mail.nobl.k12.in.us

http://north.noblesvilleschools.org (School Web site)

http://www.nobl.k12.in.us/media/NorthMedia/index.htm (LMC Website)

"It is our choices, Harry, that show who we truly are, far more than our abilities." Professor Dumbledore to Harry in *Harry Potter and the Chamber of Secrets* by J. K. Rowling

Carl A. Harvey II's
FAVORITE FIVE

Favorite Professional Book?
School Library Media Activities Monthly

Favorite Read-Aloud?
Watch Out ! Big Bro's Coming **by Jez Alborough**

Favorite Web Site?
http://www.school.discovery.com/schrockguide

Favorite Search Engine?
Google

Favorite Company?
Kids Ink (a great local children's bookstore!)

Lifesaver Tool 78. Favorite Five, Carl A. Harvey II

GO PUBLIC!

Carol Faas, Media Specialist

Professional Experience

- Two years as media specialist at M. K. Rawlings Elementary School, Gainesville, Florida (also worked as a media aide while completing M.Ed. program)

- Twenty years as a technical writer

Honors

- 2001 Literacy Award for Rawlings Elementary School (Florida Reading Association)

- Vice-president of Alachua County Professional Association of Librarians and Media Specialists

- 2002 presenter at Florida Association of Media Specialists (FAME)

- Recognized by Gainesville Area Chamber of Commerce for Outstanding Fundraising Efforts

- Recipient of nineteen grants (including one of seventy-five nationwide Federal Library Grants!)

Lifesaver Tips: Best Practices:

- Market Your Library!

   "Last year, my first year, my circulation more than doubled—something of a miracle for a school where 96 percent of the students are on free lunch! In addition, our reading scores went way up. How did I do this? First of all, I got kids to come into the media center—this was the first hurdle. It was the worst media center in the county when I took over. I cleaned and redecorated the place, did free family portraits on Open House night, brought in my pug dog for a reading buddy and did "book ads" with my dog in the class-rooms. I wrote grants (nineteen!) and bought so many books. I started the Accelerated Reader Program. I use my background in marketing and public relations to market books to kids."

- Advice to Newbies

  "This is a really creative job. Don't be tied into what your predecessor did. Find some teachers who share the same interests and work closely with them. Realize that you can't make everybody happy. Also—this is important—make up detailed orders all year long so that when the frenzy of spending Title I money hits in May, you're ready to go! Any time you have money to purchase teacher requests, do so! This makes teachers in-credibly happy. Visit the school bookkeeper every morning and every afternoon to make sure he or she pushes those purchase orders through—some school bookkeepers respond better to the person standing in front of them—be that person!"

- It's a Laugh

  "I did a big public relations blitz all year long, including television news spots for reading. I had a blonde streak, and I was wearing a leopard-print scarf during one TV ap-pearance. That morning several students came into the media center and said they saw me on TV. With tones of great admiration, they said, 'Mrs. Faas, you look just like Cruella de Ville!"

- Last Words

  "Use your free, local resources! I started a monthly performing arts series. I invite my friends to come to school and perform in the media center. I can fit about four classes in at a time. I host folksingers, violinists, lighting experts, pilots—whoever will come for free! This doesn't cost the school a penny and it's great publicity for the school—often appearing in the local news and papers!"

Lifesaver Trip 79

faas2@gru.net

http:www.sbac.edu

"If you ask for something, you will get it!"

Carol Faas's
FAVORITE FIVE

Favorite Professional Book?
I refuse to choose just one! I like the general theme of
intellectual curiosity.

Favorite Read-Aloud?
Books in Spanish and English—especially those that
can be sung

Favorite Web Site?
http://www.sptimes.com and http://www.upi.com

Favorite Search Engine?
Ask Jeeves

Favorite Company?
Follett by far!

Lifesaver Tool 79. Favorite Five, Carol Faas

PICKY ABOUT YOUR LIBRARY? SO'S HICKEY!

Mary L. Hickey, Media Specialist

Professional Experience:

- Fourteen years as media specialist in Bibb County, Georgia

Honors

- Scholarship to Pursue National Board Certification

Lifesaver Tips: Best Practices

- Literacy

    "This is so basic and simple that it seems unimportant—but it is absolutely vital! I have worked in schools with very low test scores and literacy rates. Any way I can help students learn to read—and enjoy what they read—is critical! Things as simple as giving book markers to students who can read the name of their books sends a message that reading is important!"

- Creative Solutions

    "I soon found that, to be successful in this job, I would need to come up with solutions for those small, annoying problems that can lead to big resentments. The first problem was the pencil problem. Students come from somewhere else—normally without pencils. Or students break pencils on purpose so they can get up and sharpen the broken pencil (go figure!). Or they insist on erasing when taking notes, when a line drawn through would take care of the mistake. My solution? I buy dozens of what our warehouse calls first grade pencils. They are not as fat as the primary pencils from kindergarten, but are thicker than number two pencils. They also do not have erasers. I keep them in a mug on a shelf, and they never get stolen. No one wants them. I loan them to whole classes who come in for research—or to students who want get up and sharpen.

A second problem I found was students wanting to use the restroom. As soon as one goes, they all have to go! My solution? Students who must use the restroom give up their book check out to go. When they realize they have to give up their book, 98 percent of the students decide they can wait after all!"

A third, and final, solution is to the problem of students who don't want to take notes. My solution? I store clipboards from the dollar store neatly in a basket near the computers. These clipboards provide a flat, sturdy surface (students can even take notes while sitting in a circle on the floor!). When using the clipboards, students seem more focused, on task, and even more studious—I promise!"

- Creative Cataloging

"I have worked in Title I schools that have lots of 'stuff.' Rocks, magnets, measuring containers, scales, thermometers, incubators. . . . But teachers could never remember who had what, or where it was and we lost track of equipment when teachers moved or changed grade levels. I created a section called 'Curriculum,' and catalogued the stuff according to Dewey number. For example, rulers and scales: Cur 389 Rul; Rocks: Cur 551 Roc. Teachers were willing to give up what they had when they knew they would be able to retrieve it—or find it—when needed."

- Advice to Newbies

Talk to teachers
Establish media committee and rally for their support
Don't attempt too much too fast
Enlist your principal's support (If that's impossible, at least keep him or her informed!)
Decide what is most important and stick to it (Remember, you can't do everything!)

Lifesaver Trip 80

smmccp6@cox.net

http://www.bib.k12.ga.us/brookdale/home.htm

"Any book you haven't read is a new book!"

Mary L. Hickey's
FAVORITE FIVE

Favorite Professional Book?
Jim Trelease's Read Aloud Handbook

Favorite Read-Aloud?
Chicka Chicka Boom Boom **(K)**
Maniac Magee **(Fifth Graders)**
The Polar Express **(any grade at Christmas!)**
Mama, Do You Love Me? **(Primary)**

Favorite Web Site?
My son's!

Favorite Search Engine?
Google

Favorite Company?
Follett and Bound to Stay Bound

Lifesaver Tool 80. Favorite Five, Mary L. Hickey

SS 9

HEAD SWIMMING?
GET ORGANIZED!

GET CARDED!

My partner, Kaaren, is truly the best acquisitions librarian I have ever seen. She has elevated the process of ordering books to an art form. Because she only orders "the best of the best" based on starred reviews, our media center boasts of having the best collection around (eat your heart out, public library!). Using Kaaren's cards can help you deal your library a winning hand.

Lifesaver Tips

- To save money, write on the flip side of those millions of leftover card catalog cards you haven't known what to do with! (These cards also make great scrap paper.)

- Go through your reviews and write cards for books you want to order.

- Most jobbers, like Follett and Baker & Taylor, only require the title and author.

- Kaaren recommends also jotting down the ISBN number to ensure you get the right book.

- Compile the cards, wrap a rubber band around them, and send them off to a Free Order Typing Service (Follett and Baker & Taylor) pay postage, too.

- When you receive the typed list back, double check the cards to make sure everything is in order.

- If everything appears correct, send in the order.

- Keep cards in alphabetical order (by title or author) in the format that works best for you.

- Keep a card catalog file drawer of cards "To Be Ordered," "On Order," and "To Reorder."

- When you get the books, simply place the card in the front of the book. Any remaining cards are for backordered, out of print, or out of stock books you may want to reorder.

- Kaaren's card system is an easy way to keep track of books ordered, eliminating costly duplicates—a bad word according to Kaaren!).

- No need to shuffle cards—they stay neatly in order until all books are dealt.

Lifesaver Trip 81: Follett's Web Site

http://www.flr.follett.com/

Follett's site now has a Curriculum Titlewave. Those of you who have used Library Titlewave know how great it is. Now you can match your library collection to the curriculum and your state and national standards. Do the wave! (This lifesaver is dedicated to Mr. David Horton, our awesome "Follett guy" who passed away this year. Mr. Horton, who never forgot a name, will be sorely missed!)

KAAREN'S KEEPS
BEST BOOKS LIST

Created by Kaaren Baumgartner, Media Specialist, Ben Davis High School

Booklist Cumulative Index: February 15 and August issues

Booklist Top of the Lists: January 1 and 15 issues

ALA Notables: Booklist, March 15 issue

Booklist Editor's Choice: January 1 and 15 issues

School Library Journal's Book Prices (replacement cost for lost or damaged books): March issue

School Library Journal's Best Books of the year: December issue

Booklist Top Black History Titles: February 15 issue

ALA Notable Children's Films, Videos, Recordings, Computer Software, and Computer Web
    Sites: March 15 issue

School Library Journal's Cumulative Index: December issue

IRA-CBC Choices: Reading Teacher, October issue

Instructor Magazine's Year Best Choices: May–June issue

Time Magazine's Best Book of the Year: third week of December issue

New York Public Library List of 100 Recommended Titles Booklet: January (has been $4;
    check with Office of Branch Libraries)

School Library Journal's Children's Books in Spanish: February, May, and November issues

School Library Journal's Reference Books: February, May, August, and November issues

School Library Journal's December Holiday Books: October issue

School Library Journal's Cumulative Indexes Online: www.SLJ.com

School Library Journal's Criticas; English speaker's guide to the latest Spanish language titles:
    accompanies April, June, August, and December issues

School Library Journal's Trade Newly Available in Paperback: May and November issues

Get Carded Again!

Kaaren's Cards for Computer Management

Are you tired of trying to keep track of all those serial numbers, models, and endless supply of numbers you inherit every time you get a new computer? Our school has an online work order system. Any time you have a problem with a computer, you fill out a work order online and e-mail it to Andy, our awesome computer specialist. Although an extremely efficient system, the work order also requires the user to supply serial numbers and models with each repair request. Kaaren has come up with an easy way to keep on top of computers—especially when it seems they are always being shuffled around. To keep a full hand and keep our computers "straight," we use Kaaren's Cards for this, too.

Lifesaver Tips

- Again, recycle old card catalog cards for this procedure.

- Begin by making a map of your computer lab or media center computers (we had a student create our map on a computer; see Lifesaver Tool 82).

- Number each computer on the map.

- Make copies of the map and place it on the wall next to the computers.

- For each computer, make a card denoting the assigned computer number (from your map), brand, serial number, monitor, and other pertinent information you need for inventory or repairs.

- Keep cards together in a file drawer. When you have a problem with a computer, refer to your map, get the computer's number, and pull out the matching card. Voila! All the information you need is at your fingertips.

- Although filling out the cards takes some time, when the process is done, you'll save tons of time later! I'll wager you may even have time to work on your computer.

Lifesaver Trip 82:
Ten Handy Tips

http://www.worldstart.com/tips/

This site has ten handy tips to help you manage your computer. Includes everything from learning how to cut and paste to saving paper by printing only what you need. Includes archive of even more helpful tips. Who knows? You may not need to fill out that computer repair card after all.

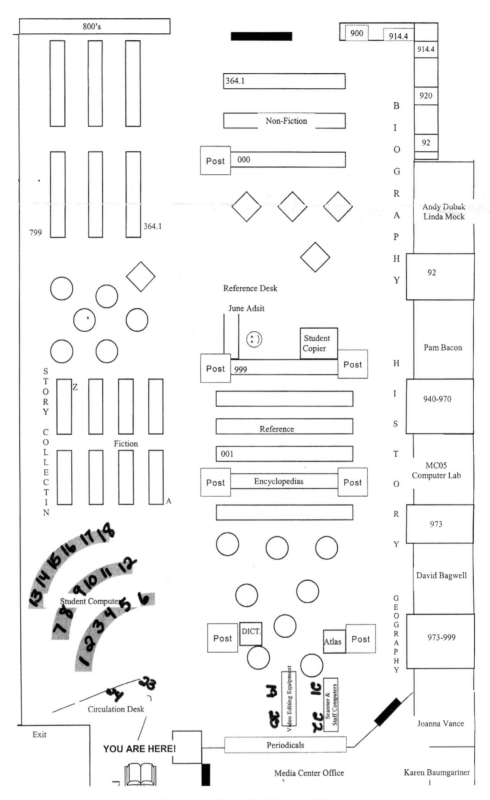

Lifesaver Tool 82. Library Map

Note: Library map designed by Jennifer Kopsas.

CALM AND COLLECTED! EASING COLLECTION MANAGEMENT

Collection management is important. In fact, it may even be the most important job in the school library media center. Still, this task often gets the least amount of attention when we try to juggle our increasing demands. So how can you manage to stay calm, cool, and collected? This collection of tips and tools may help.

Lifesaver Tips:
Four Sources to Help You Stay Calm and Cool on Collections

- **Don't have a clue about collection development?** *Collection Development for a New Century in the School Library Media Center* (Greenwood Publishing Group, 2002) can help. Lukenbill's new book provides an important overview of issues and problems in collection development and includes proven strategies for solutions. From policy to tools for selection, this book includes everything you need to know concerning collection development!

- **Don't have a collection development policy?** Check out Debra Kachel's book, *Collection Assessment and Management for School Libraries* (Greenwood Press, 1997). This book features the theories behind collection management, written collection development policies, and even worksheets to help you assess your current collection.

- **Have a collection development policy that needs revised?** Log on to http://msl. state.mt.us/slr/cmpolsch.html. Montana State Library's article "Collection Development Policy Guidelines for School Library Media Programs" offers a thorough, comprehensive checklist to ensure your policy is worth the paper it's written on.

- **Have a collection development policy that omits electronic information?** The face of collection development and management is changing. A big part of collection management is now electronic. Read "Electronic Reference—The School Library Revolution" by John M. DeBroske (*The Bookmark* 50, pp. 19–20). Another excellent source for electronic collection management can be found in Laurel Clyde's "Extending the School Library Collection—Electronically" (*Teacher Librarian* 29, pp. 41–3).

Lifesaver Trip 83:
Collection Development Training

http://www.dlapr.lib.az.us/cdt/intro.htm

This site, sponsored by Arizona State University, is for librarians and others new to collection development. Includes an overview of collection management, policy information, and even a community survey for assessment purposes. Easy to navigate and one you'll want to keep in your collection—electronic!

LIBRARY MEDIA CENTER COLLECTION MANAGEMENT

Managing our Library Collections for Information Power	Document created by Bellingham public schools http://www.bham.wednet.edu/library/tablec.htm
Assess	*Know what you need* 　Identify collection needs 　Conduct an annual inventory
Acquire	*Know how to select and acquire what you need* 　Identify high-quality materials that meet district guidelines. 　Select and order materials for purchase based on criteria. 　Follow established ordering procedures. 　Process new materials. 　Review the process by which a parent or guardian can request reconsideration of instructional materials.
Maximize access	*Know how to bring people and resources together* 　Provide a welcoming, helpful environment for all patrons. 　Maximize search capabilities for users. 　Publicize diverse resources. 　Eliminate physical, intellectual and time barriers as far as possible.
Maintain	*Know how to keep collection current and functional* 　Care for library resources. 　Eliminate materials that do not conform to district guidelines. 　Produce records of collection maintenance and development. 　Follow acceptable alternatives for dealing with lost or damaged materials. 　Perform occasional housekeeping chores on the collection.

Lifesaver Tool 83. Library Media Center Collection Management

Library media center management chart, http://www.bham.wednet.edu/library/table.htm. Used with permission.

YOU'VE GOT A DATE! MANAGING A CENTRAL CALENDAR

Do you often wish there was more time in a day? Well, from what I've read, it's not always more time that's needed—it's really more efficient time management. I'm learning (the hard way!) to manage my time and be more effective. I hope these tips are "timely" for you as well!

Lifesaver Tips

- **C** **Check your calendar!** Before agreeing to a meeting, dinner invitation, or doctor appointment, check your calendar carefully. I don't know how many times I've had to call and reschedule just because I didn't bother to check first. Rescheduling wastes valuable time. Try to do it as seldom as possible!

- **A** **Allow extra time between appointments.** Unless holding back-to-back appointments is to your advantage, allow extra time between appointments. You never know when a meeting will run over or you may want to get a cold drink before moving on to the next meeting.

- **L** **Learn to use one calendar.** Learn to use one calendar. By keeping personal and work appointments on the same calendar, you won't double book yourself or find yourself rushing off to your child's sporting event at the last minute.

- **E** **Enter all dates and appointments immediately.** By entering all dates immediately in your calendar, you'll save time spent having to search your office or home for that scrap piece of paper that holds a critical date or meeting time. A common time management practice stresses never touching a piece of paper twice. Deal with it the first time you see it—don't keep shuffling it around.

- **N** **Never forget a birthday again!** Keep your address and date book with your monthly calendar. At the beginning of each month (or each year, if you're compulsive, like me), write down upcoming birthdays and anniversaries. By writing important days on the calendar you review daily, you'll never forget an important day again.

- **D** **Don't agree to a meeting when the time is inconvenient.** Although simplistic, this practice can save valuable time. For example, if you know you have to be at the education center next Friday for a meeting, why go this Friday too? By arranging multiple meetings on the same day and at the same location, you can save time and not have to run back and forth.

- **A** **Always enter events in pencil.** The only constant is change—use pencil!

- **R** **Run off copies of your calendar for staff.** By making copies of your calendar for other staff members, your team can be more productive and aware. If you don't want your staff to know of personal items, just place a small "Post-it" over confidential items before photocopying. You won't waste time calling your assistant to tell her you'll be out—she'll already know!

Lifesaver Trip 84: Franklin Covey

http://www.franklincovey.com/

The definition of organization is Franklin Covey! Go to this site for time management organizers, tools, and workshops.

Want to Get Organized?
It's a Date!

➢ At-A-Glance

http://www.ataglance.com

A discount place to purchase At-A-Glance products is
http://www.officeworld.com/*

➢ Day Runner

http://www.dayrunner.com

Log on to this site each day for a planning tip.

➢ Day-Timer

http://www.daytimer.com

This site offers beginners a step-by-step guide to building their
Day-Timer planner.

➢ The Priority Planner

http://www.fluttersoftheheart.com/planners.shtml

This less well-known site offers customizing options—buy just what
you need.

NO MORE MEDIA MAID!

Picture this. You've got a teaching license, a master's degree in library science, ten years of teaching experience, countless hours of professional development training—but still you find yourself picking up trash that students leave in the computer lab. If this sounds familiar, refocus and take aim. The key? Use strategies that get students in the picture!

Lifesaver Tips

- Post a laminated checklist in each computer lab (Lifesaver Tool 85A).

- Post an enlarged checklist on the computer lab door.

- With the help of your technology guru, design computer wallpaper listing student expectations. For example, "Shut Down Computer When Done" or "Log Off Computer and Push in Chair."

- Post a notice on the door to let the last teacher in the lab know they are responsible for closing down the lab (Lifesaver Tool 85B). Just having the teacher's name posted makes that teacher more accountable for the lab.

- Post your school's technology rules in each lab (Lifesaver Tool 85C) for easy reference. For example, when "No Games" is clearly posted, the students have no excuse for playing arcade games in their free time.

- Enlist the support of your administration. For example, our school just implemented a "Three Strikes You're Out!" policy with the computer lab. If the lab is left in poor condition, that teacher gets a strike. After three strikes, the teacher is not allowed to sign up for the computer lab. It would be impossible to put a policy such as this into place without the support of the administration.

Lifesaver Trip 85:
Leadership Issues in Educational Technology

http://ef004.k12.sd.us/leadership_issues_in_educational.htm

A one-stop shopping source for technology-related issues ranging from creating acceptable use policies to strategies to utilize technology to improve learning. If you want to get your school on the same page with technology, start here!

PERSONS SIGNED FOR THE COMPUTER LAB ARE RESPONSIBLE FOR THE LAB

COMPUTER LAB CHECKLIST

1. **NO** Food or Drink allowed in the Lab.
2. Before leaving the Lab:
   a. Log off computer
   b. Straighten workstation
   c. Throw away all trash and papers
   d. Push in all chairs

Last class on the schedule, which is posted on the door, is responsible for shutting down the computers and monitors before leaving.

Teachers: Please inspect the room before leaving so that the room is acceptable for the next group.

THANKS!
Media Maid!

LIFESAVER TOOL 85A. Computer Lab Checklist

Last Person Scheduled for Lab:

Please shut down all computers! Thanks!

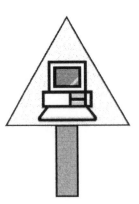

LIFESAVER TOOL 85B. Computer Lab Notice
Graphic by Christopher Duncan.

STUDENT COMPUTER POLICY
SCHOOL YEAR _____

The use of computer technology at our school is a privilege that comes with responsibility. Failure to abide by the following guidelines may result in your losing the computer privilege.

1. Do not attempt to modify the appearance or operation of any computer. This includes but it not limited to commands, copying or installing software, or copying files of any type. Every computer should remain in the default configuration.

2. Tampering with or vandalizing hardware, software, or data will not be tolerated. It is each student's responsibility to check the computer each day before and after use and to report problems immediately.

3. No diskettes or CD-ROMS unless specified by the teacher.

4. Games that are not directly related to course curriculum are forbidden.

5. No student is to use a computer without an authorized staff member present. This includes before school, after school, during lunch, and all other times.

6. No food or drink is allowed near a computer.

7. A student must save files in his or her directory on the server. Any files stored on the hard drive will be erased. Files should not be downloaded from the Internet.

8. A student may only use approved software.

9. The student is responsible for his or her own password and should change it whenever necessary for security reasons. A student may log in using only his or her user ID and password, which must be kept confidential.

10. A student should never attempt to access files of another student.

11. No e-mail.

12. Only authorized students may use the Internet.

13. A student using the Internet may visit only teacher-approved sites.

14. No Web sites should be printed without teacher approval.

15. The Internet is for educational use only!

I understand that if I violate any of the rules stated above or perform any other disruptive technology-related actions, I will be subject to loss of computer and/or Internet use. Other possible consequences include loss of a grade or suspension. I further understand that I will be financially responsible for the repair or replacement of stolen or abused hardware, software, or materials.

_____	_____	_____	_____
Signature	Printed Name	Date	Grade

LIFESAVER TOOL 85B. Student Computer Policy

WORK ORDER WOES

Having a system for handling computer repairs can help you—and your computer guy (Hi, Andy)—get organized! Say goodbye to work order woes and hello to organization!

Lifesaver Tips

- Photocopy the Work Order Form in Lifesaver Tool 86 and place in a convenient spot.

- This form can easily be put online.

- Save copies of all work orders submitted to avoid duplication.

- This system can be adapted for a variety of needs. For example, a work order system could be created for information needs. Teachers and students could submit their needs manually or electronically.

Lifesaver Trip 86:
Online Work Order Example

http://www.uml.edu/Dept/WE/deptserv/comprep.htm

A simple example of an online work order that "works!"

WORK ORDER FORM

Computer Department Only:

WORK ORDER

LEVEL OF IMPORTANCE:

___ Critical—Now!

___ Important—Today or Tomorrow!

___ Soon—This Week!

___ When Convenient—No Hurry!

Name:_____

Room number:_____ Department:_____

Phone number:_____ E-mail:_____

Room/computer number where problem is occurring:

_____

_____

_____

_____

Description of problem:

_____

_____

_____

_____

Resolution of problem:

_____

_____

_____

_____

Date closed:_____

Comments: _____

Lifesaver Tool 86. Work Order Form

Library Lifesaver 87

GRAB A TIGER BY THE TAIL!

As I was researching time management techniques and organizational strategies on the Internet, I came across an advertisement claiming that, with this product, you could "Find Anything in Five Seconds or Less—Guaranteed!" Needless to say, I was intrigued and more than a little skeptical. I clicked on the link and became convinced enough to try a free thirty-day trial of the Paper Tiger. Find out how to grab your own tiger by the tail and get started clearing out your own jungle of paperwork. I'm not "lion," either!

Lifesaver Tips

- The Paper Tiger allows you to organize anything—mail, computer software, pictures, videotapes—by attaching a number to it.

- A variety of keywords assigned to the documents allow you to retrieve it more quickly than with traditional alphabetical filing systems.

- A built-in reminder system helps you meet deadlines.

- No more time is wasted trying to find something buried in a stack on your desk.

- Try the program free for 30 days without obligation to buy.

- Get free technical support at (800) 430-0794.

Lifesaver Trip 87: The Paper Tiger

http://www.thepapertiger.com/

A guaranteed solution to your paperwork problems. Thanks to this Tiger, your office will no longer be a jungle!

Ten Tips for Making Your Life
Less Stressful and More Productive

Taming the Paper Tiger is not just a software program—it's a complete methodology you can use in all aspects of your personal and professional life. Consider these possibilities:

1. Continually eliminate clutter from your life. Practice The Art of Wastebasketry®. Ask yourself, "What's the worst possible thing that could happen if I didn't have this?" If you can live with your answer, toss it!

2. Clutter Is Postponed Decisions. Organize the top of your desk: In Box for papers you haven't looked at (not a place for postponed decisions!). Out Box for things you need to take someplace else. File Box for papers to file in places you can't reach from your desk.

3. Sort papers/e-mail using The FAT System: File, Act, Toss. Organize files into two types: Reference Files (things you don't know if you will need, but are afraid to toss) and Action Files (things you need to do or delegate).

4. Utilize a database program, such as Outlook or Act!, for storing names and contact info.

5. Store all the electronic data you create in one electronic folder, such as My Documents. Then name documents with a series of key words and phrases (up to 255 characters). Use the Search feature of your computer to quickly find electronic files—just like Paper Tiger!

6. Create templates and checklists for things you do repeatedly so you are not constantly re-inventing the wheel. (Packing lists, meeting planning, etc.).

7. Make a list of the best results you want each day.

8. Don't be afraid to ask colleagues and supervisors for help when you run into a problem. Frequently something that is difficult for you to do is easy for someone else—and vice versa. You will get the best results if you focus on what you do best!

9. Implement the "Just in Time" reading method. Instead of creating a pile of publications to read someday, quickly scan the table of contents for articles of interest. Then use The Paper Tiger software to file them quickly so you can access them by keyword when need to read them.

10. Continually ask yourself "Is this the best use of my time right now?" Use your Paper Tiger Action File Index as a powerful tool to make sure you working on your most important projects.

Barbara Hemphill is the author of Kiplinger's *Taming the Paper Tiger at Work* and *Taming the Paper Tiger at Home*, *Simplify Your Workday* and coauthor of the new book *Love It or Lost It: Clutter-Free Forever.* Her company, located in Raleigh, North Carolina, assists individuals, families, and organizations in creating and sustaining a productive environment so they can accomplish their work and enjoy their lives. Hemphill can be reached at (800) 427-0237 or at www.ProductiveEnvironment.com.

Reprinted from "Taming the Paper Tiger" Newsletter (September 2002) by Barbara Hemphill
Lifesaver Tool 87. Ten Tips for Making Your Life Stressful and More Productive

CONQUER CLUTTER

General George S. Patton Jr. said, "We can conquer only by attacking." I believe the same is true of clutter. If you don't work diligently on clearing the clutter, the war on organization—and perhaps even productivity—will be lost. To help you win the battle over clutter, here are five sources of ammunition.

Lifesaver Tips:
Pam's Picks

Organizing Plain and Simple by Donna Smallin (Storey Books, 2002).

Written by the same author as *7 Simple Steps to Unclutter Your Life,* Smallin provides motivational tips and strategies to for organizing individual rooms, finances, time, and home life. Although chapter 18 is donated solely to work, strategies throughout the entire book are work-relevant. In addition, the author provides information on dealing with transitions, be those at home or work. A must-buy especially if you're a Covey *First Things First* fan.

Organizing from the Inside Out by Julie Morgenstern (Owl Books, 1998).

The classic of organizational books, this title has proven staying power. Also available in audio and video formats, Morgenstern provides the basic concepts of analyze, strategize, and attack to help you manage clutter and organize your life and work. The chapter "Attack: Getting the Job Done" offers space-making solutions—important in schools with cramped quarters. The section title "How Long Will It Take?" section in each chapter provides a realistic timetable for projects. Finally, Morgenstern's "Julie's No-Brainer Toss List" provides permission, encouragement, and motivation to cut the clutter. Another must-have title.

KISS Guide to Organizing Your Life by Dr. Donald Wetmore (DK Publishing, 2001).
Part of the Keep It Simple Series (KISS), this book is a thorough guide to organization and planning. The book includes a twenty-step plan for changing your life and helps you relieve stress involved with everyday tasks. The author believes all people have the ability to be successful if they manage their time differently and backs his claim up with proven solutions. A third must-have in your solutions library!

Lifesaver Trip 88:
Start Decluttering

http://wholebrainmotivation.com/clutter/goals/start.htm

A plethora of articles devoted entirely to decluttering. Includes an online newsletter subscription, articles, and a discussion group for other cluttered minds (like mine)!

TIPS FOR PAPER CLUTTER

by Rita Emmett, Recovering Procrastinator

- Feed the wastebasket

- Get rid of what you don't need

- Skim material as soon as it arrives

- Don't even skim junk mail; just toss it

- Pass on to the appropriate person any papers someone else can handle

- Find a place for everything worth keeping and put the papers where they belong

- Realize the world won't end if you get rid of it

- Recycle it

- Ask yourself: Do you really want to be the caretaker of this paper? Do you really want to devote precious space to this?

- Handle each piece of paper only once

- Get rid of it

"Tips for Paper Clutter," excerpt from *The Procrastinator's Handbook: Mastering the Art of Doing It Now*, by Rita Emmett (Walker & Company, 2000), reprinted with permission. Rita Emmett is a professional speaker and author. She can be reached at http://www.RitaEmmett.com.

Lifesaver Tool 88. Tips for Paper Clutter

WEEDING THE GARDEN

This four-letter word can be a bad word for many of us: weed! With all there is to do, it's difficult to "dig up" time to weed, but maybe you're interest in weeding will "grow" after I've planted the seed!

Lifesaver Tips

- **To pull or not to pull:** If in doubt, pull it.

- **Cover your ground:** Don't pull every book on a subject before you order new.

- **Don't plant too late:** Look at copyright dates when ordering.

- **Don't plant too early:** You may want to wait for reviews before buying.

- **Don't wear your good clothes:** It's difficult to weed in a dress—wear pants on weeding days.

- **Be prepared for rain:** It might not rain or flood (although it happened in my library!), but sometimes your weeding plans have to be postponed. Be flexible but get back to it.

- **Check for growth:** Don't wait too long before weeding. Weed often and on a regular basis.

- **Share the fruits of your labor:** Just because you don't want it doesn't mean another teacher doesn't either—have a free books cart handy.

- **Weed with a friend:** It's more fun to do it with someone. My partner and I weed every Monday like clockwork. Students and teachers have learned not to bother us when we're weeding. Although we only weed for an hour or two weekly, others know it's important, too.

Lifesaver Trip 89:
Sunlink's Weed of the Month

http://www.sunlink.ucf.edu/weed/

A site to help librarians decide what—and what not—to weed. Each month focuses on a different area of the media center. Archives are available for reviewing past months. Tips for weeding are available.

Weed the Garden:
Five Steps to Weeding Success

Step One: Look for books that are inaccurate, outdated, or misleading.

Step Two: Look critically at any books with the words "New" or "Modern" in the titles.

Step Three: Look at the content of the book, not just the physical condition, when deciding to weed (the book can be reordered or repaired if the content is good).

Step Four: Look for help. If you're not sure about a book, ask the content-area teacher—after all, they're the field experts.

Step Five: Look for support. Make sure your principal is behind your weeding efforts. When others see many books being discarded, they often become alarmed and may even complain. Be prepared and proactive!

Happy Weeding!

Lifesaver Tool 89. Weed the Garden

TAKE IT "FOUR" GRANTED: FOUR WAYS TO ORGANIZE AND MANAGE GRANTS

Are you interested in applying for grants but haven't had the time to follow through? This lifesaver can help you organize and manage your grant efforts—and hopefully make your time pay!

Lifesaver Tips: Grants—The Rules According to Boyle!

By Dr. Janet Boyle

- Rule 1. Find an appropriate source for what you want funded.

- Rule 2. Once you receive the proposal application information, follow the directions to the letter.

- Rule 3. Network—both with people and on the Internet. Many great resources and funding ideas can be picked up this way.

- Rule 4. Even if your proposal is rejected, try, try again! Success rate for a grant writer is usually 25 percent . . . but that percentage goes up and improves with each new submission. Practice makes for better proposals.

- Rule 5. If your proposal is rejected, ask for the evaluation comments. This will help you improve your future proposals!

Dr. Janet Boyle is the assistant principal for curriculum and professional development, Ben Davis High School, Indianapolis, Indiana.

Lifesaver Trip 90:
School Grants: Grants and Opportunities for K–12 Schools

http://www.schoolgrants.org/grant_opps.htm

Your one-stop site for PK–12 school grant opportunities. Don't take this site "four" granted—it's outstanding!

GRANT APPLICATION CHECKLIST— 10 STEPS FOR SUCCESS

1. Did you read the application carefully? _____

2. Did you attach all requested information? _____

3. Does your need match the grant goals/guidelines? _____

4. Does your grant have an evaluation piece? _____

5. Is your grant realistic? _____

6. Did you have someone objective edit or proofread? _____

7. Did you save a completed copy for your files? _____

8. Did you sign and date the final draft? _____

9. Did you send the grant via certified mail? _____

10. Did you make your principal aware you were applying? _____

Remember: Even excellent grants can be turned down because of $!

Lifesaver Tool 90. Grant Application Checklist—10 Steps for Success

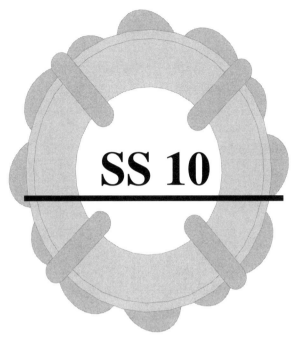

SS 10

SAIL INTO TECHNOLOGY—
TECHNOLOGY TOOLS

THE BEST SHOT ON DIGITAL CAMCORDERS

Gone are the heavy, bulky video cameras of yesteryear. Those dinosaurs have been replaced by their small, snappy cousins—digital camcorders. But which one should you buy? Let's find out, future filmmakers!

Lifesaver Tips

- Digital Camcorders come in two formats: MiniDV or Digital 8.

- Prices range from $500 to $2,000.

- Most weigh less than two pounds.

- No more loss of quality when you copy videos—digital video retains its original quality.

- Features to look for include LCD (liquid crystal display) viewer, autofocus, image stabilizer, and quick review.

- Pick Three: Consumer Reports Top Three Camcorder Recommendations

  – Sony's DCR-PC110 ($1,800)
  – Panasonic's PV-DV951 ($2,300)
  – Hitachi's DZ-MV100A ($1,999.95)

- For complete results, see "Home-movie Options" in the November 2001 issue of *Consumer Reports*.

Lifesaver Trip 91:
DV Spot: Digital Camera Resource Home Page

http://www.dvspot.com/

Focus on more digital camcorder recommendations here!

Robie Martin's

TECHNOLOGY TOOLBOX

Tool: Digital Video Camera

Tip: Hit Me with Your Best "Shot!"

As part of our school's eighth-grade promotion ceremony, we show a student-produced video, highlighting students' activities throughout their academic careers. To obtain the raw footage we need to create the video, I train my student library aides to use the digital video cameras. Teachers and staff now know to call the library and inform us of upcoming events so that we can put them on our schedule and be prepared to shoot at any time. The student aides use a checklist to ensure that every student is included in the video. They have creative license over what it will look and sound like (although I retain editorial rights!). The end result is a wonderfully fun, student-created keepsake of their years at our school. It is now a popular tradition !

Robie Martin is the media specialist at Parsons Middle School, Parsons, Kansas.

Lifesaver Tool 91. Robie Martin's Technology Toolbox

TURNING PAGES ON E-BOOKS

Since I began experimenting with e-books (specifically the Rocket eBook Reader) about three years ago, things have really improved. Unfortunately, e-books for the Rocket eBook (now known as Gemstar) are becoming increasingly difficult to find. E-books in other formats, such as MS Reader, are now much more readily available. In addition, you can use MS Reader e-books on any computer—you don't need a specific handheld gadget (like the Rocket eBook Reader) to get started. All you need is the following information!

Lifesaver Tips

- Download Microsoft Reader on up to four desktop, laptop, or Pocket PC computers for free (http://www.microsoft.com/reader/downloads/pc.asp).

- Microsoft Reader has a text-to-speech feature (students can hear the words as they read the computer screen) also available for free download.

- Get support for Microsoft Reader and answers to frequently asked questions (FAQs) here! (http://www.microsoft.com/reader/support/pc/default.asp).

- Love classics? Get 1,800 free e-book downloads from the University of Virginia's Ebook Library (http://etext.lib.virginia.edu/ebooks/ebooklist.html).

- Pick Three: Places to purchase e-books for the MS Reader

  – Ebooks.com (www.ebooks.com) offers a wide range of professional, academic, and popular titles, as well as an e-mail update subscription to notify readers of new and upcoming releases.

  – Powell's Bookstore (http://www.powells.com/ebookstore/mreader.html) is one of the few places to purchase titles for the Rocket eBook (aka Gemstar).

  – When you join eBook Club (http://www.ebookmall.com) for $19.95, you can download up to one thousand titles. You can't go wrong here!

- If you still want a handheld e-book reader, I suggest the Palm Pilot (www.palm.com) or the Handspring Treo that's an all-in-one phone, organizer, and Web browser (www.handspring.com).

Lifesaver Trip 92:
Free E-Books Directory

http://www.free-ebooks.net/

A "priceless" site for more free books!

Jamen McGranahan's

TECHNOLOGY TOOLBOX

Tool: E-Books

Tip: Turning Pages on E-Books

Our school uses e-books to supplement our media center collection and provide our patrons with a means to read a book online.

We've downloaded the MARC records for the e-books into our catalog so that they are readily accessible (one search brings up both print and electronic resources).

E-books are well received by our students on campus. In fact, one of their recommendations from last year was for us to add more!

Jamen McGranahan is the systems services librarian at Waggoner Library/Trevecca Nazarene University, Nashville, Tennessee.

Lifesaver Tool 92. Jamen McGranahan's Technology Toolbox

DIGITAL CAMERAS—
THEY'RE A SNAP!

Digital cameras are everywhere! And why not? They're fun, easy-to-use and, as time goes by, increasingly more affordable. There are so many models to choose from, but these tips will help you focus on the right camera!

Lifesaver Tips

- Digital cameras operate by memory so you have no film to mess with.

- Digital pictures are transferred directly to your computer.

- Digital pictures can be printed on photo paper (available at retail stores), eliminating expensive and timely processing delays.

- Digital pictures can be easily edited and e-mailed to friends and family members.

- Leading brands are Kodak, Nikon, Olympus, and Sony.

- The more "pixels" a camera has, the sharper the images will be.

- The price of the camera depends on the amount of pixels.

- Digital cameras have a variety of ways to save photos, such as a memory stick, floppy computer disk, and even CD-RW (CD rewriteable) disks. Although I prefer regular 3.5-inch floppy disks, the choice is up to individual users.

- Consumer model digital cameras range in price from $100 to $1,000.

- Must-have features to look for include autofocus, zoom lens, and automatic flash.

- Nice-to-have features include red eye reduction and optimum memory.

- Pick Four (plus a bonus pick!):

    – Canon PowerShot G1 at $800 (3- and 4-megapixel range)

    – Olympus Camedia C-2040 Zoom at $500 (2-megapixel range)

    – Toshiba PDR-M61 at $300 (2-megapixel range)

    – Sony Mavica at $900 (2-megapixel range)—my recommendation!

- For more complete information, see "Megapixel Matters" in the November 2001 issue of *Consumer Reports*.

Lifesaver Trip 93: All Digital Photography

http://www.alldigitalphotography.net/

Amateur and veteran photographers can find all the lessons and tips needed to operate a digital camera. "Shoot!" I wish I'd known about this site sooner!

Pamela S. Bacon's
TECHNOLOGY TOOLBOX

Tool: Digital Cameras

Tip: Digital Cameras Are a "Snap!"

I love my Sony Digital Mavica Camera! In fact, I love it so much that when my first one was stolen, I chose to buy the exact same camera to replace it. One of my most successful digital camera projects has been our school's Student of the Month display. Each month after the winners are announced, I take pictures of the students and then insert the pictures into a PowerPoint presentation. Sometimes I'll just print the presentation to post on a bulletin board. Other times I'll give it to our radio-TV-film guy (Hi, Jon!) to display on our television scrolling announcements. Either way, the project is a "snap" to put together with this great camera!

Lifesaver Tool 93. Pamela S. Bacon's Technology Toolbox

KNOW IT ALL ABOUT SMARTBOARDS

I've used SMART Boards, but I still have a long way to go before I'm at the implementation stage with this tool. For this lifesaver, I'll be learning right along with you! What is the phrase? "Work smarter, not harder!"

Lifesaver Tips

- The SMART Board is an interactive whiteboard.

- It allows you to control computer applications (or write notes) simply by pressing on the board's touch-sensitive surface.

- Standard dry erase markers are used to write on the board, and notes can be saved to a computer file for future use.

- The SMART Board is a perfect classroom and library tool for presentations, allowing teachers to demonstrate CD-ROMs or Internet sites easily to an entire classroom at once.

- Although the SMART Board is available in three sizes, the SMART Board 560 (the middle option) is a good choice for classrooms and computer labs.

- Four colors of stylus pens come with the board.

- SMART Boards are extremely durable—studies have shown some schools are still using their 1989 models!

- SMART Boards can be easily cleaned with any recommended product.

- Studies show that SMART Board can increase student motivation to learn by as much as 50 percent. (Study conducted by Michael J. Weimer, West Noble Middle School, Ligonier, Indiana. Full report can be found at www.smarterkids.org).

Grants are available for SMART Boards—go to http://www.smarterkids.org for complete information!

- Pick Three:

    – Smart Board 580 at $1,399 (72" display)

    – Smart Board 560 at $1,119 (60" display)

    – Smart Board 540 at $700 (47" display)

Lifesaver Trip 94:
SMART Board Distributors

http://www.smarttech.com/where/displaywtb.asp?jumplist=IN&x=17&y=10

"Learn" where to purchase a SMART Board in your state!

Linda Sears's

TECHNOLOGY TOOLBOX

Tool: SMART Boards

Tip: Know It All about SMART Boards

We got our SMART Board this year, and I used it for library media center orientation. I prepared a PowerPoint presentation, using digital pictures focusing on several aspects of our library media center. I also scanned in pictures from last year's activities to give students a better idea of what goes on in here. Then I burned the PowerPoint onto a CD so students entering the school later in the year would receive the same basic information.

I also used the SMART Board to explain the Accelerated Reader Program to students and varied it slightly for parents on PTO Night. The SMART Board makes it so much easier to see and to move from page to page within a presentation.

Linda Sears is the library media specialist at Oak Mountain Intermediate School, Birmingham, Alabama.

Lifesaver Tool 94. Linda Sear's Technology Toolbox

TECHNOLOGY—IT'S IN THE PALM OF YOUR HAND!

I've had my Palm Pilot IIIC for almost two years. Although I can't yet state that I'd choose my Palm over a good, old-fashioned paper calendar, I must admit this new little gadget is growing on me. Here are some tips before you "take off" with your Palm!

Lifesaver Tips

- Convenience—with my all-in-one calendar, there's no need to keep both a home and work calendar.

- Portability—I always have my telephone and address book with me.

- Synching options—I can sync calendars with coworkers, bosses, and my teenage son (who thinks he's the boss!).

- Communication—I can write anywhere and I never forget my to-do lists.

- Reminders—with the alarm option, I no longer forget (or even worse, miss) a meeting.

- Our school is a Palm School, so I had no doubt about which device to purchase. There are, however, several good handhelds, or PDAs—personal digital assistants— (e.g., Handspring's Visor Edge or Compaq's iPaq), now on the market.

- Pick Three:
    – Palm m105 at $200 (best all-around organizer w/o phone option)
    – Palm m500 at $400 (best computer substitute)
    – Palm m100 at $130 (best basic organizer)

Looks like the Palms have it!

Lifesaver Trip 95: Palm Home Page

http://www.palm.com

With reviews like Palms get, this site's a thumbs up!

Diane Mentzer's
TECHNOLOGY TOOLBOX

Tool: Palm Pilots

Tip: Technology—It's in the Palm of Your Hand!

I use my Palm Pilot as a gradebook. I have a special gradebook program on it where I keep my attendance and record forgotten books at the beginning of each class. I grade papers at my desk and then hot sync the information into my computer in my office. This system allows me to grade students as they are participating in activities. The extra mobility also allows me a way to record behavior problems as they happen. I'm responsible for giving grades to my students during the second and fourth marking periods, and the Palm makes this task manageable. Using a Palm is much more convenient than dragging around my laptop!

Diane Mentzer is the library media specialist, technology coordinator, and Webmaster at Paramount Elementary School in Hagerstown, Maryland.

Lifesaver Tool 95. Diane Mentzer's Technology Toolbox

THE 1, 2, 3s ON LCDs

In my media center, selecting an LCD was not an easy task. The first hurdle I had to overcome was that I am surrounded by glass, and, as a result of the glass, I'm surrounded by glare. The second hurdle was the inability to turn off the lights to show a presentation. I learned that for best results, an LCD has to have an extremely high number of lumens, thus raising the cost significantly (my Dukane was $5,000). In most cases, an LCD does not have to be that pricey, and the good news is that, like all technology that's been available for a while, prices have decreased significantly. Presenting your options . . .

Lifesaver Tips

- Why use an LCD? Because you can present colorful, attention-getting electronic presentations with minimal effort.

- The brighter your room, the higher number of lumens you'll need—800 lumens is the average.

- If you plan to keep the lights on, you'll need at least 1,000 lumens.

- Ease of use is a factor you'll want to consider. Most projectors come with two cables: a power cord and a cord to attach the projector to your computer. Whenever possible, try out the LCD before purchasing to ensure that it's easy to set up and connect.

- Portability may be a factor to consider if you plan to travel with the LCD device or use it around the building. Projectors can weigh anywhere from two to ten pounds.

- Although lightweight projectors are easy to carry, the trade-off can come in terms of picture quality.

- If you plan to move your projector often, an extra sturdy case is a necessity.

- The number of colors from projector to projector does not vary—all have 16.7 million colors—not your average Crayola box!

- All projectors are both Mac and PC compatible, thus computer compatibility isn't a concern.

- A remote control is a nice-to-have feature for presentations.

- Searching the Web for bargains is a great idea before you buy. Hundreds of sites are available, but here are two I found: http://www.adtech-sys.com/content/specials.asp and http://www.priceshock.com/hardware-projectors-lcd-projectors.html.

- For more complete information, go to http://www.dukane.com/AudioVisual/products/HowLCD.htm or http://www.aviinc.com/projectors-plasmas/bestsellingprojectors.asp.

- Pick Three:

    - Sony VPL-CX4 at $3,699

    - NEC LT240 at $3,195

    - Epson America at $2,516

Lifesaver Trip 96:
AudioVisual Innovations Frequently Asked Questions

http://www.aviinc.com/projectors-plasmas/faqs.asp

Answers to sixteen FAQs about projectors. For example, What do I if "my projector is not working when I turn it on?"

Dr. Kathleen Revelle's
TECHNOLOGY TOOLBOX

Tool: LCD Projectors

Tip: The 1, 2, 3s on LCDs

One lifesaver I have just begun to use may be "old hat" to others. My principal had an LCD projector that he used to display PowerPoint presentations for faculty meetings and other events. Most of the time, though, the projector was stored on the floor of his closet. I now house the LCD in the library and use it at least once a week to demonstrate computer-based lessons. Just this past week, for example, I used the projector to introduce sixth- and eighth-grade students to the basics of PowerPoint. In addition, I was able to demonstrate search techniques in Gale databases for tenth- and twelfth-grade students. Although this tip doesn't have "bells or whistles," it works! Now, when the principal needs the projector, he or she just comes and checks it out from the library!

Kathy Revelle is the media specialist at Buffalo Academy for Visual and Performing Arts, Buffalo, New York

Lifesaver Tool 96. Dr. Kathleen Revelle's Technology Toolbox

AN "A" FOR ALPHASMARTS

I can't say enough good things about these little guys! AlphaSmarts work as well for high school kids as they do for elementary students. These word processors are durable, lightweight, and affordable at only $250 each. After these tips, you'll know all the answers to make the "smart" choice for you!

Lifesaver Tips

- The AlphaSmart home page is http://www.alphasmart.com/.

- Purchasing options include individual AlphaSmart units (with or without rechargeable batteries and the Infrared "beaming" option).

- AlphaSmart classroom bundles are also available. Bundles feature thirty AlphaSmarts with a rolling, powered storage cart.

- The newest AlphaSmart, the Dana, is now available. The Dana has a larger screen than traditional units and includes the Palm operating system—making it an excellent, affordable laptop alternative.

- The basic AlphaSmart runs about $200 per unit.

- AlphaSmart with rechargeable batteries and infrared capability costs $250 per unit.

- The Dana model, because of its additional features, costs $399 (or less if for quantities of thirty or more).

- Classroom Bundles (thirty units with charging storage cart and all cables) costs about $6,700 with IR and Rechargeable battery features.

- Software such as AlphaQuiz, Inspiration Outlining, and AlphaWord are available for free downloading and upgrading from the Web site.

- AlphaSmart support includes a technical support hotline, a newsletter, and an online community to discuss technical issues, lesson plans, purchasing choices, and more.

- Test drives are available for AlphaSmarts. You can borrow a unit for two weeks free of charge!

Lifesaver Trip 97:
Paula Whitmer's Practical Classroom Activities with an AlphaSmart

http://itech.fcps.net/alphasmart%20activities.htm

The "smart" idea is to get started "write" away!

Pamela S. Bacon's
TECHNOLOGY TOOLBOX

Tool: AlphaSmarts

Tip: An "A" for AlphaSmarts

I started out with five AlphaSmarts and was so happy with the little word processors that I bought thirty more!

My high school students love using AlphaSmarts. When we finish a story, I'll hand out an AlphaSmart to each group. Then I have the group work together to answer the questions at the end of the story. One group member is responsible for typing the answers. All other group member s are responsible for editing. I find the answers to be more thorough and complete simply because the students type them on the computer!

I also loan AlphaSmarts to students on an overnight basis. For students who don't have a computer, the durable, lightweight units are the perfect answer!

Lifesaver Tool 97. Pamela S. Bacon's Technology Toolbox

LEAPFROG—HOP TO IT!

My twin sister, a principal at a K–2 building, told me about this great tool. Because I now teach at the secondary level, I didn't even know LeapPads existed. Not only a great technology tool for education, they're just plain fun. Students will jump for joy when they use these in your elementary media center!

Lifesaver Tips

- LeapPad is an interactive learning tool that brings books to life.

- LeapPad encourages individualizes learning—readers learn and read at their own pace.

- LeapPad teaches phonics, spelling, and vocabulary skills.

- LeapPad makes reading a game with hands-on activities, games, and stories.

- The LeapPad library includes interactive books and magazines.

- With an optional MindStation connector, unlimited activities can be downloaded from the Internet.

- How does it work? The reader places a book or magazine on the LeapPad. When the user places the LeapPad stylus on a word, the device reads the word aloud.

- Different leap levels are available. For example, a kindergarten student might read the Leap 1 books, whereas a second-grader might read the Leap 2 choices.

- For older students, in upper elementary and junior high (for remediation), the QuantumPad works the same way.

- Although recommended for younger readers, either the LeapPad or QuantumPad would work nicely for English as a Second Language (ESL) students or for struggling readers.

- Finally, for middle and high school students, the IQuest has a variety of subject-related quizzes and even standardized test (SAT, PSAT, ACT) materials.

- By going to the LeapFrog schoolhouse (http://www.leapfrogschoolhouse.com), educators can get special discount pricing and read research findings about all LeapFrog products.

Lifesaver Trip 98:
BizRate.com

http://toys.bizrate.com/marketplace/search/search__cat_id—14011000,keyword—LeapFrog,mid—17968.html

Get an annotated list of the LeapFrog library here!

Marilyn Loop's
TECHNOLOGY TOOLBOX

Tool: LeapFrogs

Tip: LeapFrogs: Hop to It!

I have been using LeapFrog every day in the library since last spring. We currently have a large quantity of the product, and my teachers and I all love it. Because we do not have a public library nearby, I check out LeapPads with headphones and up to three books per week to parents. Many parents use it to read with their children when they are unsure of how to speak the language or are not good readers themselves. This product, which enhances traditional phonics instruction, is a wonderful product for teachers, parents, and students. My second-language students (and parents!) can use the LeapPad to help with the articulation of sounds. I have also used the LeapMat in my library to help teach the concept of alphabetical order and placement of books on shelves. I can't say enough about this wonderful product!

Marilyn Loop is the library media specialist at Elaine Wynn Elementary School in Las Vegas, Nevada.

Lifesaver Tool 98. Marilyn Loop's Technology Toolbox

SCANNING THE OPTIONS

Okay, I'll admit it! The scanner scares me. I don't know why, but this technology tool and I don't see eye to eye! So, what did I do? I did what every smart media specialist does when she doesn't know something about technology—I asked a student!

Lifesaver Tips (Learned the Hard Way!)

- A scanner comes with scanner software to install on your computer.

- Scanners can scan text (using OCR—optical character recognition—software) for e-mailing, faxing, or editing later.

- Scanners can scan pictures—the most popular option.

- Most scanners include both OCR software (to read text) and photo editing software (like PhotoShop) to edit and manipulate pictures.

- When you activate your scanner (by clicking on the scanner icon or the computer or by pushing the button on the scanner itself), your scanner software pops up.

- The scanner will then ask you what type of document you are scanning and where you want to save your document (see Lifesaver Tool 99).

- When scanning photos, it's best to save them as a .jpg or a .bmp file; these are the most universal, thus allowing almost everyone to open them.

- Scanning takes lots of patience and practice—have fun and smile!

- When purchasing a scanner, you want to look at the dpi (dots per inch). As usual, the higher the number, the higher the price.

- For more information, refer to "Scanners Get Cheap," *Consumer Reports* (May 2001; see Lifesaver Trip 99 for information on accessing *Consumer Reports* online).

- Pick Three:

    – Agfa SnapScan e20 at $65 (600 dpi)

    – Epson Perfection 640U at $150 (600 dpi)

    – Cannon CanoScan N65OU at $100 (600 dpi)

    – Honorable Mention: HP Scanjet 5550C at $299 (12–999,999 dpi)

Lifesaver Trip 99:
Consumer Reports Online

http://www.consumerreports.org

Information on scanners—and everything else—from a name you can trust. It's now online and better than ever! Some information is available for free; subscribers, however, have full access to articles and information for $24 per year or $4.95 per month.

Nancy R. Kellner's

TECHNOLOGY TOOLBOX

Tool: Scanners

Tip: Scanning the Options

I use a scanner (Apple's Color One Scanner 1200/30) to reproduce characters from the book *Five Creatures* by Emily Jenkins. I then laminate them and place Velcro tabs on the back. Next, I make a simple Venn diagram on my felt board and I place the characters in the appropriate place on the diagram for each page of the book. After we finish with this activity, the class and I make up new scenarios with the characters.

(In the past, I've also made Venn diagrams out of hula hoops to teach the concepts of grouping and regrouping!)

Nancy R. Kellner is a librarian at Marguerite E. Peaslee School in Northborough, Massachusetts.

Lifesaver Tool 99. Nancy R. Kellner's Technology Toolbox

YOUR "STANDARD" TECHNOLOGY TOOLS

Now that you've found out about all these great technology tools, you may want to begin using them right away. Before you grab your toolbox, you'll need the nuts and bolts of technology standards.

Lifesaver Tips: National Educational Technology Foundation Standards for All Students

- Basic operations and concepts

    1. Students demonstrate a sound understanding of the nature and operation of technology systems.

    2. Students are proficient in the use of technology.

- Social, ethical, and human issues

    1. Students understand the ethical, cultural, and societal issues related to technology.

    2. Students practice responsible use of technology systems, information, and hardware.

    3. Students develop positive attitudes toward technology uses that support lifelong learning, collaboration, personal pursuits, and productivity.

- Technology productivity tools

    1. Students use technology tools to enhance learning, increase productivity, and promote creativity.

    2. Students use productivity tools to collaborate in constructing technology-enhanced models, prepare publications, and product other creative works.

- Technology communications tools

    1. Students use telecommunications to collaborate, publish, and interact with peers, experts, and other audiences.

    2. Students use a variety of media and formats to communicate information and ideas effectively to multiple audiences.

- Technology research tools

    1. Students use technology to locate, evaluate, and collect information from a variety of sources.

    2. Students use technology tools to process data and report results.

    3. Students evaluate and select new information resources and technological innovations based on the appropriateness for specific tasks.

- Technology problem-solving and decision-making tools

    1. Students use technology resources for solving problems and making informed decisions.

    2. Students employ technology in the development of strategies for solving problems in the real world.

"National Educational Technology [NETS] Standards for Students," International Society for Technology in Education (2002). All rights reserved. Reprinted with permission. To find out more, go to http://cnets.iste.org/sfors.htm. To order "NETS for Students: Connecting Curriculum and Technology," books which include grade-specific standards, call (800) 336-5191.

Lifesaver Trip 100: NETS Lesson Plans

http://cnets.iste.org/search/s_search.html

A searchable database of lessons in all subject areas correlated with the technology standards—a great safety net!

TECHNOLOGY PLANNING TOOL

Use Lifesaver Tool 100 to start your lesson tune-ups. The tool provides a place to note which forms of technology you'll be using and, even more important, which standards you'll be targeting. With today's high-stakes testing, technology can help you to ensure your students' achievement.

Title:
Curriculum:
Grade Level Span:

Purpose:

Description:

Activities:

Technology	Curriculum Standards	NETS for Students

(Continued)

Tools and Resources
(List all Web sites, specific software and hardware needs)

Assessment
(How will you assess the students' learning? If you have a rubric, record it here.
Be as specific as possible.)

Authors (including contact information)
(Record the names and email addresses, if possible, of those who contributed to the development
of this lesson sequence)

Personal Account
(Have you taught this lesson sequence before? What are the great learning/experiences you had?)

Lifesaver Tool 100. Technology Planning Tool

BIBLIOGRAPHY

Alborough, Jez. *Watch Out! Big Bro's Coming!* New York: Scholastic, 1997.

Albright, Michael, Susan Zvacek, Sharon Smaldino, and Michael R. Simonson, editors. *Teaching and Learning at a Distance: Foundations of Distance Education.* Upper Saddle River, N.J.: Prentice Hall, 1999.

Aylesworth, Jim. *Old Black Fly.* New York: Henry Holt, 1992.

Bacon, Pamela S. *100 Library Lifesavers: A Survival Guide for School Library Media Specialists.* Englewood, Colo.: Libraries Unlimited, 2000.

Bannister, Barbara F. *Elementary School Librarian's Survival Guide.* New York: Center for Applied Research in Education, 1993.

Basso, Michael J. *The Underground Guide to Teenage Sexuality.* Minneapolis, Minn.: Fairview Press, 1997.

Bear, John, and Mariah Bear. *Bears' Guide to the Best Education Degrees by Distance Learning.* Berkeley, Calif.: Ten Speed Press, 2001.

Bear, John, and Mariah Bear. *Bears' Guide to Earning Degrees by Distance Learning.* Berkeley, Calif.: Ten Speed Press, 2000.

Burton, Virginia Lee. *The Little House.* Boston: Houghton Mifflin, 1942.

Carle, Eric. *The Very Hungry Caterpillar.* New York: Scholastic, 1987.

Chute, Alan G., Melody M. Thompson, and Burton W. Hancock. *The McGraw-Hill Handbook of Distance Learning.* New York: McGraw-Hill, 1999.

Clements, Andrew. *Frindle.* New York: Aladdin Paperbacks, 1998.

Cline, Foster, and Jim Fay. *Parenting with Love and Logic.* Colorado Springs, Colo.: Navpress, 1990.

Consumer Reports Buying Guide 2000. Yonkers, N.Y.: Consumers Union, 1999.

Cooper, Gail, and Garry Cooper. *New Virtual Field Trips.* Greenwood Village, Colo.: Libraries Unlimited, 2001.

Covey, Stephen R. *First Things First*. New York: Simon & Schuster, 1994.

Cronin, Doreen. *Click, Clack, Moo: Cows That Type*. New York: Scholastic, 2000.

Dawes, Chip. *Ocp: Oracle9i Certification Kit*. Alameda, Calif.: Sybex, 2002.

Deedy, Carmen Agra. *The Library Dragon*. New York: Scholastic, 1994.

Eisenberg, Michael. *The Big 6 in Secondary Schools*. Worthington, Ohio: Linworth, 2000.

Encyclopaedia Britannica Print Set and Yearbook. Chicago: Encyclopaedia Britannica, 2001.

Fay, Jim. *Teaching with Love and Logic*. Golden, Colo.: Love & Logic Press, 1995.

Gordon, David T. *Digital Classroom: How Technology Is Changing the Way We Teach*. Cambridge, Mass.: Harvard Education Letter, 2000.

Grisham, John. *A Painted House*. New York: Dell Publishing, 2001.

Information Power: Building Partnerships for Learning. Washington, D.C.: American Library Association, 1998.

Johnson, Dave, and Rick Broida. *How to Do Everything with Your Palm Handheld*. Berkeley, Calif.: McGraw-Hill Osborne, 2001.

Joose, Barbara M. *Mama, Do You Love Me?* San Francisco: Chronicle Books, 1991.

Kachel, Debra. *Collection Assessment and Management for School Libraries*. Westport, Conn.: Greenwood Press, 1997.

Kimmel, Eric. *I Took My Frog to the Library*. New York: Scholastic, 1990.

Lau, Linda K., editor, and Salomon Smith Barney. *Distance Learning Technologies: Issues, Trends and Opportunities*. Hershey, Pa.: Idea Group Publishing, 2000.

Lindbergh, Anne Morrow. *Gift from the Sea*. New York: Vintage Books, 1975.

Lukenbill, W. Bernard. *Collection Development for a New Century in the School Library Media Center*. Westport, Conn.: Greenwood Press, 2002.

Martin, Bill. *Chicka Chicka Boom Boom*. New York: Aladdin Paperbacks, 1989.

McGraw, Jay. *Life Strategies for Teens*. New York: Simon & Schuster, 2000.

Mehrotra, Chandra Mohan, C. David Hollister, and Lawrence McGahey. *Distance Learning*. Thousand Oaks, Calif.: Sage Publications, 2001.

Milam, Peggy. *InfoQuest: A New Twist on Information Literacy*. Worthington, Ohio: Linworth, 2002.

Morganstern, Julie. *Organizing from the Inside Out*. New York: Owl Books, 1998.

National Educational Technology Standards for Students: Connecting Curriculum and Technology. Eugene, Ore.: ISTE Publications, 2000.

The New Oxford American Dictionary. New York: Oxford University Press, 2001.

Palloff, Rena M., and Keith Pratt. *Building Learning Communities in Cyberspace*. San Francisco: Jossey-Bass, 1999.

Peet, Bill. *How Droofus the Dragon Lost His Head*. Boston: Houghton Mifflin, 1971.

Rathman, Peggy. *Officer Buckle and Gloria*. New York: Scholastic, 1995.

Rowling, J. K. *Harry Potter and the Chamber of Secrets*. New York: Scholastic, 1997.

Shan, Darren. *Cirque du Freak: The Vampire's Assistant*. Boston: Little, Brown and Company, 2001.

Sherry, L., and Morse, R. An assessment of training needs in the use of distance education for instruction. *International Journal of Educational Telecommunications* 1, no. 1 (1995): 5–22.

Smallin, Donna. *Organizing Plain and Simple*. North Adams, Mass.: Storey Books, 2002.

Spinelli, Jerry. *Maniac Magee*. New York: Harper-Collins, 1992.

Stevenson, Nancy. *Distance Learning Online For Dummies*. New York: John Wiley and Sons, 2000.

Tovani, Cris. *I Read It, but I Don't Get It*. Portland, Maine: Stenhouse Publishers, 2000.

Trelease, Jim. *The New Read-Aloud Handbook*. New York: Penguin Books, 1989.

Van Allsburg, Chris. *The Polar Express*. Boston: Houghton Mifflin, 1985.

Wetmore, Donald E. *KISS Guide to Organizing Your Life*. New York: DK Publishing, 2001.

Williams, Marcia L., Barbara Covington, and Kenneth Paprock. *Distance Learning: The Essential Guide*. Thousand Oaks, Calif.: Sage Publications, 1998.

World Almanac and Book of Facts. Mahwah, N.J.: World Almanac Press, 2002.

World Almanac for Kids. Mahwah, N.J.: World Almanac Press, 2002.

Wyeth, Sharon Dennis. *Something Beautiful*. New York: Doubleday Books for Young Readers, 1998.

Index

About the Author

PAMELA S. BACON is Library Media Specialist, Southmont High, Indiana, and a freelance writer.